Praise for
The Pressure's Off

"If, like me, you see blessing-centeredness rather than God-centeredness as a great weakness of American evangelicalism, you will hail this exploration of the freedom and joy of grace as timely therapy, a word in season that we all needed. May it be widely read and thoroughly digested."

—J. I. PACKER, theologian and author of *Knowing God*

"The evangelical church, choking under a pervasive legalism/moralism that suffocates the human spirit, finds a powerful voice for freedom in Larry Crabb. Writing from the inside out, he presents a vibrant way of living with passion and without pressure."

—BRENNAN MANNING, author of *Ruthless Trust*

"C. S. Lewis wrote about prosperity knitting us to this world, and while we are seeking our place in the world, the world is actually finding its place in us. Dr. Larry Crabb has constructed a compelling narrative that shows how we have imprisoned ourselves by using the world's ways to 'get something from God,' instead of appropriating God's way to receive something from Him."

—CAL THOMAS, syndicated columnist and author

"Dr. Crabb not only gives us a clear mandate to celebrate Christian freedom, he also is our accompanist and exemplar on the Way of Freedom. You know he has walked that way with you. A remarkably personal message."

—JAMES M. HOUSTON, Chancellor Emeritus and professor
of Spiritual Theology, Regent College, Vancouver, B.C.

"This book makes a very important statement about how to live the Christian life. It takes the Christian beyond the obstacles and disappointments and, above all, beyond the age-old enemy of self straight into the arms of grace. Once there, the pressure is off. A real worthwhile read."

—FRANK RETIEF, Presiding Bishop,
Church of England in South Africa

"At last we have a book that confronts contemporary Christian culture with its increasing tendency to be taken up with blessings more than the Blesser. I doubt whether anything Larry has ever written, or may write in the future, will contribute more powerfully to the needs of modern-day Christians than *The Pressure's Off.*"

—SELWYN HUGHES, director of the Center for World
Revival and author of *Every Day with Jesus* devotional

WEARY?

CAN'T GET IT RIGHT?

STRUGGLING TO MAKE LIFE WORK?

The

THERE'S A *NEW WAY* TO LIVE

PRESSURE'S
OFF

WORKBOOK

LARRY CRABB

WATERBROOK
PRESS

THE PRESSURE'S OFF WORKBOOK
PUBLISHED BY WATERBROOK PRESS
2375 Telstar Drive, Suite 160
Colorado Springs, Colorado 80920
A division of Random House, Inc.

ISBN 1-57856-553-7

Printed in the United States of America
2002—First Edition

10 9 8 7 6 5 4 3 2 1

CONTENTS

Questions You May Have About This Workbook

What will *The Pressure's Off Workbook* do for me?

This workbook will help you discover and understand what the Bible calls "the new way of the Spirit." As Dr. Larry Crabb writes in *The Pressure's Off*, "This new way leads through a life that doesn't work very well into a mysterious certitude that anchors us in storms of doubt, into moments of ecstasy that keep bigger hopes alive when good dreams die, into the terrifying experience of death to self that allows our true selves to walk out of the tomb into the light of day."

Is this workbook enough, or do I also need the book *The Pressure's Off*?

Your best approach is to read the book *The Pressure's Off* as you go through this companion workbook. However, many key portions from the text of *The Pressure's Off* are included here to give you a sufficiently broad and accurate indication of the book's content.

If you do decide to read *The Pressure's Off* as you go through this workbook, you'll find the appropriate chapters to read listed at the beginning of each weekly lesson.

The lessons look long. Do I need to work completely through each one?

This eight-lesson workbook is designed to promote your thorough exploration of each week's material, but you may find it best to focus your time and discussion on some sections and questions more than others.

Also, you may decide to follow a slower pace than one lesson per week. This could be true whether you're going through the workbook individually or in a group. In a group that meets weekly, for example, you may decide to spend two weeks of discussion time on each lesson. (In your first meeting, decide together on what you believe to be the best pacing and schedule.) If you're going through the workbook on your own, you may simply want to try completing two or three questions each day.

Above all, keep in mind that the purpose of the workbook is to help guide you in specific life application of the biblical truths taught in *The Pressure's Off.* The wide assortment of questions included in each weekly lesson is meant to help you approach this practical application from different angles and with expansive reflection and self-examination.

Allowing adequate time to prayerfully reflect on each question will be much more valuable for you than rushing through this workbook.

Fellow seeker, will you dare to imagine
what for so long you've feared may not be available?
Will you join me, a trembling pilgrim,
in putting aside the cynicism that skillfully avoids the risk of hoping?
Will you embrace your desire for the one thing you would give all else to gain—
an actual encounter with Jesus Christ, now, before heaven?

—from the opening pages
of *The Pressure's Off* by Dr. Larry Crabb

OLD WAY OR NEW WAY?

*This week's lesson is based on
the introductory content
("A Parable: Night Question"
and "Introduction: Two Paths")
plus Part I: "There's a New Way to Live."*

As you begin each week's study, remember to ask for the Holy Spirit's help in hearing and obeying His words for you at this time.

Included in each weekly study you'll find a number of excerpts from the book *The Pressure's Off,* each one marked at the beginning and end by this symbol: 📖. These excerpts serve not only to convey Dr. Crabb's message from the book, but also to stimulate your reflection and discussion and to guide your exploration of Scripture. The excerpts are usually brief, so you may want to frequently refer back to the book *The Pressure's Off* and review their fuller context.

1. At the beginning of *The Pressure's Off* is a section entitled "A Parable: Night Question." Near the end of this workbook it's reprinted in full (beginning on page 133). Read this short section now.

Think about the beginning mind-set of the woman in this parable. What appears to be her view of God and her overall view of life?

If I am good enough I will be blessed & things will go the way I think it should

How would you summarize what happens to the woman in this parable?

She is shown the difference between her way - trying to control her life by doing what is right & trusting God in whatever circumstances

In your own words, how would you express the message or "point" of this parable?

TWO PATHS

In his introduction to *The Pressure's Off,* Dr. Crabb describes two paths and what it's like to walk each one. He writes that all of us are always walking one or the other of these two paths—and that we're doing so "right now, at this very moment."

2. Below are several lines of description that Dr. Crabb gives for what it's like to walk one or the other of these two paths. How closely does each statement match the path you seem to be on at this moment? Rate each statement from 0 to 5—the higher the number, the more closely the description matches your life at present.

   _0_ You've decided that what you most want out of life is within your reach, and you're doing whatever you believe it takes to get it.

   _2_ Your life is filled with pressure. Inside, where no one sees, your soul is weary. You see no way to step off the treadmill.

   _4_ Life is going well, and you're satisfied. But you sense something's wrong, something's missing. The pressure is still there.

   ___ You've realized that what you most want is beyond your reach, and you're trusting God for the satisfaction you seek. You want Him. Nothing less, not even His blessings, will do.

   ___ You have hope. Your soul may be weary, your interior world may be filled with struggles no one sees, but you have hope. At times you rest.

   ___ Something is alive in you; the desire of your heart is not smothered. You can taste freedom. And the taste brings joy.

3. In the preceding question, the first three descriptive statements have to do with the "Old Way," an approach to living that Dr. Crabb describes and exposes in many ways throughout *The Pressure's Off.* In the book's introduction, he

says that "most people live the Old Way all of their lives" and that "most people who go to church live a religious version of the Old Way." He also writes this:

> 📖 The Old Way involves a quid-pro-quo arrangement with God or, if not with God, then with the order in the universe, with the rules that make life work. If you do what you should, then you get what you want, either from a moral God who rewards good behavior or from an orderly world that you effectively use. It leaves you in control of how things turn out in your life. The Old Way promises a better life filled with good things that make you happy.
>
> But it never delivers, though it may seem to for a long time. The Old Way doesn't work for one reason: You never keep your end of the bargain, not completely. No one does. 📖

At this point, how strongly do you agree with Dr. Crabb's conclusion that the Old Way "never delivers"?

It's true Because we (I) never fulfill my end completely

What questions do his comments raise in your mind?

None right now

4. At this point in his discussion, Dr. Crabb introduces the phrase *Law of Linearity*—"a law that states there is an *A* that leads to the *B* you want. Figure out what *A* is, do it, and you'll have the life you most desire. The pressure's on." This Law of Linearity, he says, is a belief held by people who follow the Old Way.

To what degree have you believed in this Law of Linearity in your own life? *In some respects . I have to be really good to get to heaven, God is mad at me when I mess up which is pretty often*

Dr. Crabb states that belief in this law brings pressure to our lives. What pressure does it bring? And is this pressure good or bad, according to your understanding of it? *Feel we (I) have to control every thing + I can't make any mistakes which of course is impossible*

5. The "New Way" is in stark contrast to the Old Way, and those who live the New Way follow a different law:

> 📖 People who live the New Way believe the *Law of Liberty*. They come as they are. They do not bathe before they approach God. They come to God for the bath. They feel no pressure to change either their inner life or their outer life, but they *desire* change in both spheres. And they are eager to do whatever will create the opportunity for change, even if it means dipping themselves seven times in a muddy river or marching around an enemy's wall for

Do not live for a better life in this world

seven days and blowing trumpets. They live for the truest desire of their hearts: to know God and to enjoy Him. They do not live for a better life in this world. And when their life here is hard, when things fall apart, they most clearly reveal who they are. They're citizens of another world who most want what this world can never provide. So they wisely indulge their deepest desire and trust God to reveal Himself to them. That's the Law of Liberty. 📖

Describe here the ways in which this description matches your own spiritual desires and longings.

RULES TO LIVE BY

📖 I have no strategies in mind to give you a better marriage, better kids, a more complete recovery from sexual abuse, or quicker healing after your divorce. Nor, I believe, does God.

I want all these things for you. So does God. And I want a better life for myself. So does God. *But He wants something more for both of us.* And only when we pursue the more will He grant the less. Or He might not. 📖

6. As you consider carefully the preceding quotation, what questions come to your mind? In what respects do you agree with what these paragraphs have to say about God? *God is the one in control + he does not always grant our wishes*

If you agree with the central message in those paragraphs, what do you think is the "something more" God wants for us?

What Scripture passages and teachings can you think of to support your conclusion about this "something more" that God wants for us?

    📖 I'm troubled by how unquestioningly we live out our determination to make this life work. All our hopes for happiness are bound up in it. It's as if we believe this is the only world we ever plan to inhabit. 📖

7. Ask yourself to what extent your hopes and expectations for happiness are bound up in this life rather than in your eternal life. As you honestly face this issue, what kind of observations come to mind?

8. Dr. Crabb affirms that the Old Way's Law of Linearity "sometimes works." How have you seen it working in your own life?

9. "We all want our lives to work well," writes Dr. Crabb, "to become better than they are or to remain as good as they are." But the problem comes, he says, "when that desire becomes our goal, the objective we most value.... Our lives then become a sustained effort to discover and follow whatever principles will provide a life that lets us feel pretty good."

Here's the result:

📖 You might end up farther from God. And you *will* end up farther from God if you think of these principles as methods to produce the better life you want. 📖

How would you explain in your own words the point Dr. Crabb is making here, as it relates to your own life?

📖 When we live to make this life work, whether we follow natural wisdom or biblical principles, we become either proud or discouraged, self-congratulating or self-hating. 📖

10. Think back to some moment when you experienced either self-congratulating pride or self-hating discouragement. To what extent can you recognize that this may have been caused simply by your commitment "to make this life work"?

OUR SET PATTERNS

📖 I lead a linear life. I want this life to work, and I'm willing to do whatever it takes to make it happen. No wonder I feel so much pressure and struggle with so much disillusionment and doubt. When things work well, I publicly say, "Praise God," and privately whisper, "Of course. I did what I was told. I got it right." When things go poorly, I publicly declare, "God is working for my good. I will trust Him"; privately I wonder, "What did I do wrong?" 📖

11. In what ways, if any, does the description in the preceding quotation reflect your own experiences, past or present?

12. Think carefully about the following words from the author.

> 📖 Let me propose a radical thought: *Maybe we have it all wrong!*
> Maybe the Christian life is not about "doing right" to "get blessed."
> Maybe the Christian life is not about the blessings of life we so badly
> want and doggedly pursue. Maybe our obedience and faithfulness are
> to be energized by a very different motive than receiving the good
> and legitimate blessings we long to experience in this life....
>
> The spiritual journey is *not* about living as we should so life
> works as we want. It's *not* a linear path.
>
> It's *not* about growing up into the maturity of a good self-image
> and developing the energy to do good things; it *is* about growing
> down into the brokenness of self-despair and deepening our aware-
> ness of how poorly we love compared to Trinitarian standards. It's
> *not* about working hard to get it right so we can present ourselves
> before God to receive the blessings we desire; it *is* about coming
> before Him as we are, honestly, pretending about nothing, becom-
> ing increasingly convinced that we can't get it right though we try as
> hard as we can, then listening for the whisper of the Spirit, "Wel-
> come! You're home. You're loved. You'll be empowered to speak with
> your unique voice as you hear the Voice of God singing over you
> with great love." 📖

How fully convinced are you of the accuracy and biblical soundness of the
assertions made in these paragraphs? Explain your response here:

Three Passages Tell the Story

Dr. Crabb cites three passages that he says are "representative, I believe, of the entire message of Scripture."

13. The first of these representative passages "establishes the Law of Linearity as the basis of a Better Life of Blessings from God, as it summarizes the conditions of an arrangement God put into effect with His Old Testament children."

    Here's the passage:

    > "Carefully follow the terms of this covenant,
    > so that you may prosper in everything you do."
    > (Deuteronomy 29:9)

    How would you state in your own words the core message of this verse?

    📖 But notice something easily overlooked. Once we accept this linear arrangement—*A* then *B*; you do this, God will do that—not only is the pressure on, but failure is guaranteed. We find ourselves in the same pickle as Israel: We can't keep our part of the bargain. When God instructed His people to "carefully follow the terms of the covenant," He was not setting a *fairly* high standard. He was not prepared to provide blessings to people who followed His rules *reasonably* well. The standard was perfection—perfect love for God and for others at every moment, in every interchange. 📖

14. Why do you think this aspect of the biblical Law of Linearity—that the standard is always nothing less than perfection—is "something easily overlooked," as the author explains? Why do we resist the notion that "failure is guaranteed"?

15. Now consider afresh what God did to rescue us from that guaranteed failure:

> 📖 Life under the harsh Law of Linearity would be unlivable. But if someone delivered you from that arrangement (not because the law was unfair but because you weren't good enough to keep it), if someone found a way to let you live as a beloved son or daughter of the king with a royal position established not by performance but by relationship, you would be profoundly grateful. Your one thought would be to get to know that person, to draw near to him.
>
> That story is true. It isn't a fairy tale. It happened. The Deliverer has come. 📖

This deliverance is the theme of the second representative passage Dr. Crabb highlights, a passage in which "the writer tells us that God has annulled that Law of Linearity":

> "The former regulation is set aside
> because it was weak and useless
> (for the law made nothing perfect),
> and a *better hope* is introduced,
> by which we draw near to God."
> (Hebrews 7:18-19)

As fully as you can, how would you explain the ways in which your own life is affected by the truth in this passage?

16. Dr. Crabb explains the incredible effects of our "new arrangement" with God in these words:

> 📖 Under the new arrangement, the reason for right living has changed. We no longer depend on a linear relationship between performance and blessing to arrange for the life we want. That arrangement has mercifully been declared obsolete and has been replaced by something new, something better. 📖

Why do you think this truth is so important for believers to fully and deeply understand?

DO YOU WISH TO BE ENSLAVED?

"But there are two difficulties with this new arrangement," notes Dr. Crabb.

> 📖 One, it requires us to yield control over what happens in our lives and to trust God to do whatever He thinks best. Regular quiet times and fervent prayer do not guarantee the cancer won't come

back; neither do they ensure expanded and effective ministry. We prefer to claim influence, if not control, over which blessings come our way.

Two, it's harder to enjoy God than His blessings. Offer a young child the choice of having Daddy present Christmas morning with no gifts *or* having Daddy absent and a stack of gifts piled high beneath the tree, and the child might choose the gifts. Only the mature value the blessing of *presence* over the blessing of *presents*. 📖

17. Assess those two "difficulties" as they relate to your own life. When is it hardest for you "to trust God to do whatever He thinks best"?

    To what extent do you find yourself more willing and able to enjoy God's blessings than to enjoy God?

18. "It's the situation," writes Dr. Crabb, "reflected in our third representative passage" in which "the apostle Paul expresses bewildered amazement that people who had the chance to draw near to God would value the Better Life of Blessings over the Better Hope of Intimacy and would again put themselves under pressure to 'get it right' to 'make life work.'"

Here's the passage:

> "We were in slavery
> under the basic principles of the world....
> But now that you know God—
> or rather are known by God—
> how is it that you are turning back
> to those weak and miserable principles?
> Do you wish to be enslaved by them all over again?"
> (Galatians 4:3,9)

Dr. Crabb adds the following commentary on this passage:

The word translated "principles" literally means "sequence." It's a word used by the Greeks to refer to elements in sequence like letters in the alphabet. The basic sequence that could be observed by watching how things work was not the rigid sequence of holy linearity established by God. By "basic principles of the world," Paul meant the natural order by which life could be managed, principles for effective living common to all religions and ethical systems. And their aim was always the same—to make life better.

In his teaching to the Galatians, Paul called these common principles "weak and miserable." Is this how you would describe the "principles for effective living common to all religions and ethical systems"? Why or why not?

19. Dr. Crabb concludes Part I of *The Pressure's Off* with these words:

> 📖 I devote the rest of this book to presenting the New Way of the
> Spirit in a manner that I pray will arouse an appetite for the Better
> Hope of drawing near to God. But I have no power to make that
> happen. *Holy Spirit, reveal to our hearts that, because of Christ,*
> > *the pressure's off,*
> > > *there's a new way to live,*
> > > > *and it's better than the old way.* 📖

With those words in mind, how would you express your personal goals or
expectations for the time you'll spend going through this workbook?

20. In quietness, review what you've written and learned in this week's lesson. If further thoughts or questions come to your mind and heart, you may want to write them here.

21. What for you was the most meaningful concept or truth in this week's lesson?

How would you talk this over with God? Write your response here as a prayer to Him.

A Worm in
the Apple

*This week's lesson is based on
chapter 4, "A Worm in the Apple,"
chapter 5, "What Dark Forces?"
and chapter 6, "The Left-Out Dragon."*

"Ever since Eden," writes Dr. Crabb, "people have had the unique capacity to believe they're heading north while their feet take them south. Our moral compass, the internal sense that approves or disapproves of what we're doing and where we're going, is seriously out of whack."

In this week's study we continue to explore what exactly is "out of whack" in our typical approach to the Christian life.

COME A LITTLE CLOSER

📖 With our almost limitless capacity to deceive ourselves, it's possible (and the possibility has been realized to epidemic proportions) for people to sincerely believe that they're living the Christian life when in fact they're following a highly Christianized version of the Old Way. 📖

1. As you consider what you've learned so far in this workbook, what do you think are some common ways in which Christians might deceive themselves in the manner mentioned in the preceding quotation?

2. "For years," Dr. Crabb writes, "I've held to an image of myself that made me want to go deep, but not too deep, and to be personally vulnerable, but only to a point." Listen as he further explains.

> 📖 Since graduate school days, and probably before, I've viewed myself as a shiny red apple sitting in a fruit bowl positioned on the center of a dining-room table. Look at me from a distance and you'll be drawn. The apple is big, there are no visible bruises, and it's well shaped.
>
> Come a little closer…and your impression that the apple is good fruit might be strengthened. You may want to pick it up and take a bite.
>
> If you do, you'll likely enjoy the taste. Have a conversation with me, come to me for spiritual direction, join a small group with me, combine your gifts with mine to develop a ministry—and you might conclude that indeed I'm the juicy, substantial, sweet-tasting apple I appear to be.
>
> But I know. I know what you don't know and what I'm determined to never let you discover. There's a worm in the center. A few more bites, and you'll spit me out. I must keep you from moving too close. To know me much is to like me. To know me fully will reveal how disgusting I really am. 📖

To what extent does this image of the worm in the apple also fit any image you've had of yourself?

3. The author continues his self-revelation with these observations:

> 📖 You see, there really is a worm in the apple. It's foolish to try to convince me it's a nice worm. There's no such thing. God sees it and hates it. So I should too. I know myself well enough to know I'm often self-absorbed. I hold grudges against people who harm me. I'm capable of hating others. My insecurities have less to do with a lack of needed affirmation, whether during childhood or now, and more to do with a demand that I be honored above another.
>
> Of course I have intrinsic value as a bearer of God's image. Of course I can revel in the wonder and fullness of God's love for me. Of course I'm privileged to live as someone unique, as a masterpiece-in-the-making of God's creative genius who has something of eternal significance to give to this world.
>
> But my self-hatred doesn't come from a failure to appreciate these truths. It comes from a God-denying demand that I be more special than you, that my efforts be recognized and effective, that I never be slighted or demeaned, that I have the resources to get what I want from life.
>
> My self-hatred is rooted in pride. I insist that someone see value in me, that I see value in myself. And when one or the other doesn't happen, I spin down into the abyss of wailing about life and loathing everything in it, including myself. 📖

4. How well can you relate to these personal disclosures from Dr. Crabb? In what ways—and how strongly—can you identify with what's portrayed in these words?

5. Dr. Crabb also explores another side of himself:

📖 Sometimes, like you, I stand on rock. Goodness actually comes out of me. I give for the right reasons. I love another with no preoccupying concern for myself....

I'm a mystery to myself. Sometimes the Spirit flows freely within me, and I'm full of joy and spiritual power. Other times, another source of energy takes over, and I'm out of sorts....

Sometimes I can feel the rock beneath my feet, and I stand tall in the storm. Other times I know I'm losing my balance as the sand beneath me begins to shift. 📖

Again, how well can you relate to this? In what ways, if any, does this description reflect your own experiences?

6. Then comes this confession from Dr. Crabb:

    📖 Sometimes I'm just too weary to worry which path I'm walking.

    But then I feel the pressure. I realize God has become a distant relative and I'm handling life on my own. Christ is my ticket to heaven but not my best friend. What I think represents the Spirit's nudgings only increases the pressure—"Why aren't you reading your Bible more?" "Why did you refuse to meet your friend for coffee?" "Do you think you're too important for him?"

    And then I long to live the New Way. I want to know the pressure's off. 📖

Once more, put into words your thoughts on how closely you can identify with this portrait.

At this time in your life, how strong is your desire for wanting "to know the pressure's off"?

OUR GREATEST NEED

Dr. Crabb states that "meaningful change in our culture, enduring change rooted in improved character rather than legislated cosmetic change, can come only after revival hits the church." He also says, "Revival in the church must begin with revolution in the soul."

"The order," he says, "is important."

    📖 First, *spiritual revolution* that moves us from Old Way living to the New Way; then *true revival* of safe community in our churches; and finally, a much-prayed-for *cultural reformation* where salty believers make unbelievers thirsty for Christ. 📖

Let's explore further these three things.

    📖 First, *spiritual revolution* in our interior worlds, a shift from the Old Way to the New....

Our greatest need is for a fresh encounter with God that exposes sin as repulsive and reveals as repulsive sin our determination to make this life work, no matter how spiritually we may go about it.

Our greatest challenge is to recognize the Old Way of the written code, to realize how often we live it, to see the New Way of the Spirit open before us, and to discover our consuming desire to follow that path into the presence of God....

Are we longing with relentless passion to draw near to God, are we desperately hungry to know Christ, are we listening intently for the Spirit's voice in our noise-filled lives? 📖

7. How strongly do you agree with what the author describes in the previous quotation as our "greatest need" and our "greatest challenge"?

How would you answer for yourself the questions in the final paragraph in the preceding quotation?

> 📖 Second, *true revival* in our church worlds, where the Spirit works through self-effacing leadership to release congregations to become safe communities, communities that exalt the Father, not the pastor; that center on Christ, not visible success; that listen to the Spirit, not people's expectations....
>
> We tilt at windmills when we thrust our swords at pornography, abortion, fatherlessness, and teen violence without first weeping over shallow community in our churches. When the Holy Spirit moves, He draws us together before He sends us into battle....
>
> Are we embracing the Law of Liberty by coming boldly, exactly as we are, into the divine community? 📖

8. In what ways do you either agree or disagree with the author's assertion that the Holy Spirit "draws us together before He sends us into battle"?

How would you answer for yourself the question in the final paragraph in the previous quotation?

    📖 And third, *cultural reformation* in our everyday worlds that lifts the satisfaction of virtue and humility above the thrill of achievement and power, and values right relationship with God over improved self-esteem....

    Our greatest challenge is *not* to Christianize secular culture into accepting family values and biblical morals....

    As we pray, "Thy kingdom come, Thy will be done, on earth as it is in heaven," we must not too quickly rise from our knees to get busy with kingdom work. We must for a season remain on our knees, humbled and dependent, begging the Spirit's help to realize which way we're taking. 📖

9. What is your response to the author's various statements in this quotation? Which of them do you agree most strongly with and why?

Which statements bring questions to your mind, and what are those questions?

WHAT DARK FORCES?

After setting forth our supreme need for spiritual revolution, true revival, and cultural reformation (in that order), Dr. Crabb states, "As long as my soul is ruled by a spirit that allows jealousy, judgmentalism, and general jerkiness to so easily be aroused and then to dominate, I won't be capable of worshiping God, of relating well to my brothers and sisters, or of attracting unbelievers to Christ. I will soil the Name of God by the way I live."

He then asks this:

> 📖 What dark forces sometimes rule in my interior world? What allows ugly emotions that I don't like and don't choose to develop so easily and rule so completely? 📖

10. To the best of your scriptural understanding, how would you summarize the Bible's overall answer to those questions?

11. As you read carefully the following excerpt, think in an honest way about your own personal ambitions and desires.

📖 It's a hard pill to swallow, but we must get the medicine into our souls.

When any ambition other than drawing near to God assumes first-place significance in our hearts, whether the ambition is blatantly self-serving or clearly kingdom-advancing, we're living the Old Way. 📖

In your own life, what would you say are the "ambitions other than drawing near to God" that are most likely to take on "first-place significance" in your heart?

📖 When our first-place privilege of nearness to God remains in first place, we abide in the vine; second-place desires become sought-after blessings. Then fruit grows on the branch. That's New Way living.

But the moment we let our desires for blessings become demands, the moment we expect blessings to come because we've met the requirements for God to grant them, the moment we think any blessing other than nearness to God is essential to life and is therefore promised now, we've chosen to live the Old Way.... We end up leading natural lives, lives energized by the flesh no matter how religiously disguised. 📖

12. Consider your own deepest motives and longings and your usual way of thinking about these. In your life, what is it that can cause a desire to become a demand?

When this happens—when our "desires for blessings become demands"—then according to Dr. Crabb it means that "we've forfeited the opportunity to experience supernatural reality and must now depend on our own resources to arrange for the blessings we want." Record here your response to this statement. In what ways do you agree or disagree with it?

📖 Listen to Paul speak strongly to Christians who were being influenced to measure up to certain standards in order to gain full favor with God: "Mark my words! I, Paul, tell you that if you let yourselves be circumcised, Christ will be of no value to you at all.... You...have been alienated from Christ; you have fallen away from grace" (Galatians 5:2,4).

Paul's point is this: *Christ promises no help when you make it your ultimate goal to secure certain blessings by doing good things.* You can pray and fast and attend seminars and buy books and double-tithe and refuse cable service on your television and practice contemplative prayer and never miss an anniversary or your son's ball games—the resources of the Spirit will have no value to you at all. God will not help us live the Old Way. 📖

13. Describe your response to the preceding biblical commentary from Dr. Crabb. You may want to include any additional scriptural content that supports your response.

14. In regard to these "resources of the Spirit" that are worthless when we're living the Old Way, Dr. Crabb points to "four distinct resources within us that make supernatural living possible," placed there by the Spirit:

   📖 A *New Purity* that makes us clean in God's sight even when we roll in mud;
   a *New Identity* that permits no labels other than ones like saint, child of God, beloved, and heaven-bound pilgrim to be accurately pinned on us;
   a *New Disposition* that actually prefers holiness to sin;
   a *New Power* to draw near to God as a forgiven heir who longs to behold the beauty of the Lord. 📖

   Take a moment to evaluate your life with respect to your appropriation of these resources. Which of them are you using most fully? Which of them do you need to draw upon more faithfully?

MODERN JUDAIZERS

"The modern church has been infiltrated by an updated version of Judaizers," states Dr. Crabb. They correspond to the Judaizers of the New Testament era:

📖 In Paul's time, particularly in the Galatian church, certain teachers were acknowledging that Jesus was indeed the Messiah, but then they added the idea that Christians had to conform to the law to gain full standing with God. They were encouraging Old Way living....

Paul called the Judaizers "dogs, those men who do evil" (Philippians 3:2).... They put "confidence in the flesh" (3:3); they taught from a settled persuasion that merit brought blessing in this life....

The Galatian Christians were drawn to this teaching. It returned control into their hands and restored pride in their own value....

Rather than depending on New Covenant resources that were gifted to them so they could draw near to God in perfect liberty, the Galatians were thinking it might be a good idea to get "religious" so they could enjoy superior blessings. 📖

15. In what ways do you recognize that the Old Way appeals to us by putting control into our hands and restoring pride in our own value?

📕 Listen to Paul scold the Galatians for buying into this different
view of spiritual growth:

"You foolish Galatians! Who has bewitched you? Before your
very eyes Jesus Christ was clearly portrayed as crucified. I would like
to learn just one thing from you: Did you receive the Spirit by
observing the law, or by believing what you heard? Are you so foolish? After beginning with the Spirit, are you now trying to attain
your goal by human effort? Have you suffered so much for nothing—if it really was for nothing? Does God give you his Spirit and
work miracles among you because you observe the law, or because
you believe what you heard?" (Galatians 3:1-5). 📕

16. Record here the main points you recognize in Paul's response to the Galatians
on this issue.

17. With that helpful background on New Testament Judaizers, we can better
understand those who are like them today. Listen carefully to this critique
from Dr. Crabb:

📕 Modern Judaizers assume the same law but give it a different
spin in their message to today's Christian: Now that we know God
by faith in Christ's atoning work (justification), *He's now available to
bless us,* to give us what we so badly want and what we think will
give us a sense of personal wholeness....

God is the *means* of blessing, the modern Judaizers say. Implied, but never stated, is that God Himself is not the blessing we seek. It's therefore right, and actually His plan, that we use Him to get a better life....

The error is subtle and terribly appealing....

Modern Judaizers cheapen God's eternal word by twisting it, like the serpent did in Eden. Rather than insisting that the blessings of life were indeed made available to any who kept God's law perfectly from the heart, and then teaching that Christ kept the law as a man and then was cursed in our place because we broke the law, they teach that it's possible to keep the law well enough to win the blessings we desire....

Modern Judaizers appeal to our lower nature, to our wrongheaded idea (first suggested by Satan) that blessings are to be valued above relationship with the Blesser. 📖

In what ways have you seen for yourself the influence of these modern Judaizers?

18. Dr. Crabb notes one of Paul's methods for resisting the Old Way's appeal:

📖 *Paul spoke openly about his pain,* not in complaint, but as a reminder that the abundant life of following Jesus means abundant opportunities to draw near to Him in hard times, not an abundance of pleasant circumstances and good feelings.

Listen to his words to the Corinthians, Christians who were more intent on feeling now what God promised they would feel only in heaven. "We are hard pressed on every side, but not crushed; perplexed, but not in despair; persecuted, but not abandoned; struck down, but not destroyed" (2 Corinthians 4:8-9).

Paul's life was not a pleasant experience. By *admitting* it and by abandoning all hope that it ever would be pleasant, the pressure was off to figure out some way to make life work. Paul lived to know God, not to use Him. He lived to draw near to God, to become like Jesus, to follow the Spirit, not to live a certain way that would please God enough to get Him to pour out the blessings of a better life. 📖

In what ways do you agree or disagree with the definition of "the abundant life" as given in the first paragraph of this quotation?

To what extent would you say that you, like Paul, are living "to know God, not to use Him"?

19. Think about the most meaningful concept or truth you've explored in this week's lesson. How would you talk this over with God? Write your response here as a prayer to Him.

WHAT'S SO WRONG
WITH THE OLD WAY?

*This week's lesson is based on
chapter 7, "What's So Wrong with What We Want?"
and chapter 8, "Blinding Deception."*

"What makes the Old Way wrong?" Dr. Crabb asks.

📖 Is it really *evil* to live for blessings available in this world? Or, for some unfortunate people, is it merely frustrating?

How can anyone seriously maintain that trying hard to make this world a better place for us to live is immoral, especially if we do so "Christianly," if we take no unfair advantage of others and resist the lure of illegitimate pleasures? And suppose we aim for spiritual meaning, and fill our days with ministry activities, and carefully and seriously follow biblical principles as best we can. We might corrupt the search for satisfaction into a selfish pursuit—and that would be wrong—but if we trust Christ to fill our lives with adventure and fulfillment and community, are we not walking a good path? Are we not then His disciples? 📖

1. From what you've learned and reflected upon so far in this workbook, how would you answer the questions in the preceding quotation?

SOMEWHERE ELSE THAN GOD

2. "The only consistent message coming from the world, the flesh, and the devil," writes Dr. Crabb, "is this: *Seek your deepest enjoyment somewhere else than in God.*"

   How have you seen this to be true in your own temptations to sin?

3. Think about the overall fundamental message that you've understood from the life and death of Jesus Christ. Then read these words:

   📖 Jesus came to earth to tell us He is the way, the truth, and the life. His death opened the *way* into God's presence, the greatest blessing of all. His teaching made clear the *truth* that life does not consist in a return to Eden's comforts; it doesn't even consist in graduation to heaven's bliss. True life is knowing God. Jesus said so (see John 17:1-3). And the *life* is Christ Himself, not the bread He could multiply or the corpse He could resurrect, but Him. Being in Him, having Him in us, living with His energy, chasing after His purposes, loving what He loves, seeing Him form in us until we're actually like Him—that's life. And it can be enjoyed in bankruptcy or affluence, from a hospital bed or a deck chair on a cruise ship, or when you walk out of a divorce court you never thought you'd see or into a surprise party celebrating fifty years of your wonderful marriage. 📖

How consistent is Dr. Crabb's view with your own understanding of what true life is, according to the teachings of Jesus?

4. "The Old Way sees things differently," Dr. Crabb asserts:

> 📖 "Yes, you do want Jesus. He's the one who can restore your marriage, provide great ideas on raising kids that really work, and prosper your ministry. Jesus teaches principles to live by, He offers methods to follow that will give you the life you want. What must you do to be saved from an unfulfilling life and strained relationships? What must you do to be saved from persecution and trouble? He'll tell you. Go to Him to find out what you must do to make life work!" 📖

In what ways, if any, do you recognize that these thoughts are actually opposed to the true life that Christ offers and provides?

In contrast, Dr. Crabb cites the words of Anne Graham Lotz, who after telling of hardships in her life then added, "Don't give me sympathy. Don't give me advice. Don't even give me a miracle. *Just give me Jesus!*"

Do you think it's wrong to pray for sympathy, advice, or a miracle when we're undergoing genuine hardship? Why or why not?

5. How strongly can you identify with the following feelings and experiences?

📖 But...I want my life to work. I enjoy it when it does. I hate it when it doesn't.

Only when my dreams shatter, and then only for a moment, do I sometimes feel a desire to draw near to God that I know is stronger than my desire for restored blessings. Only during specially intense times with God—rare in frequency and short in duration—do I pant after Him more than His blessings....

I say that the pressure's off.... Do I have any idea what that means? Maybe I really do value what Christ can do for me in this life more than I value the opportunity to get better acquainted with Him. Have I ever actually derived more pleasure from spending time with Him than from vacationing with my wife or watching my sons do well or holding my grandchildren? Is there really more joy in knowing Christ than in standing before large crowds and watching good things happen and making good money to boot? 📖

Record your response here:

IT CAN BE DONE

"It helps to know it *can* be done," Dr. Crabb writes, "that the way to God has been cleared, that the resources needed for the trip have been provided, and that the Spirit can stir up the waters that will carry us, like a fountain carries a leaf, into the presence of God."

He points to the experience of John, as we see it in the opening chapter of Revelation, as an example of how "supernatural reality can break into our lives and gush out of our souls."

> 📖 As John wrote about what happened, he tells us he was "in the Spirit" (Revelation 1:10)—indicating, I think, that a sense of expectancy seized him, likely after many desperate days of waiting on God to meet him on the rock he called home. 📖

6. What does being "in the Spirit" truly mean for you in your relationship with God?

📖 The apostle was an old man, living in the prison of a barren island, exiled there for the crime of preaching Jesus, eating poorly, sleeping uncomfortably, performing hard labor that not even a twenty-year-old should be forced to do, aware that the band of disciples was gone (most of them martyred), and discouraged by the spiritual condition of several local churches.

If he had followed Christ in hopes of enjoying a better life, he would by now have been sorely disillusioned. But then Christ appeared to him. Notice, however, what *didn't* happen when He appeared. Christ did not bring John a mattress. He did not spread a table with good food. He did not magically lift John off Patmos and set him on the mainland to hold seminars in Sardis and Laodicea.

What did happen was far better. The Spirit revealed Jesus Christ. I can hear John saying, "My life is miserable, but I ask not for sympathy, not for help, and not for a miracle. Just give me Jesus!" And that's what the Spirit did. It's a prayer God always, eventually, answers. 📖

7. Describe what it means for you, at this time in your life, to pray the prayer "Just give me Jesus."

An Insult to God

📖 More is available to us in Jesus Christ than we dare imagine. There's more to Jesus Christ than we've ever dreamed. We experience so little of Him when we approach Him only with requests. We taste so little of the mouth-stopping, complaint-ending, desire-deepening awe that His presence creates when we think more about our problems and how to solve them than about *meeting Him*. We experience so little of the joy that sustains us in suffering and the hope that anchors us amid shattered dreams when we come to Him looking for the pathway out of hardships instead of the pathway *into His presence*.

In his unpredictable expressions of mercy, the Spirit gives us glimpses of Christ that fill us with supernatural reality and shine a spotlight on the entrance to the New Way. 📖

8. Are you convinced that "more is available to us in Jesus Christ than we dare imagine"? Why or why not?

9. Dr. Crabb states again, "More is available to us in Jesus Christ than we dare imagine. We settle for so much less. We taste Him so little. Why?"

He begins answering that question with these words:

📖 The central obstacle to His life flowing in us and pouring from us is this: *We want something else more*. And that's evil. We want the blessings of a better life more than we desire to draw near to Jesus. 📖

He illustrates that point in this way:

📖 We're like the prodigal son telling his father, "I could care less about being with you. I just want your wealth. You can die as far as I'm concerned. *Just give me my inheritance.*"

That's the Old Way. It's not only foolish, it's evil....

Living for a better life in this world with more energy than we pursue a deeper relationship with Christ is evil.... It's an insult to God. He gives us the best heaven can offer, and we ask for something else. 📖

Why is it actually *evil* to want something else more than God?

DIFFERENT PEACE

📖 There's a peace the world gives. It's the tranquillity of a life that works reasonably well—decent relationships, adequate health, enough resources to enjoy life, meaningful work....

Jesus offers a different kind of peace. "*My* peace I give you. I do not give to you as the world gives" (John 14:27). The peace Jesus gives isn't dependent on deserved blessings. It depends entirely on the one supreme blessing He guarantees to all His followers: the opportunity to draw near to Him, to put every egg in the basket of His presence with us even when His absence is all we feel, to depend on Him to be doing a good work in us even when everything that happens seems bad. 📖

10. How would you evaluate the degree and quality of peace that you've already experienced in this world?

What kind of peace are you actually looking for? How would you describe the degree and quality of peace you most deeply long for in this world?

11. When you hear Jesus saying, "Come to me, all you who are weary and burdened, and I will give you rest" (Matthew 11:28)—what kind of "rest" do you expect to experience in coming to Him?

What does it essentially mean to you to "come" to Him?

SOWING TO THE FLESH

📖 Although it brings me to deeper levels of brokenness to say it, it must be said: *Whenever we focus on the blessings we want, even if they're worthy blessings, and study Christianity to understand how to get those blessings, we're sowing to the flesh.* We're living the Old Way. 📖

12. In regard to the legitimate blessings you want in life, do you agree that it's wrong to "study Christianity to understand how to get those blessings," in the way that Dr. Crabb means? Why or why not?

13. Consider your own observations of contemporary Christianity as you read these words:

> 📖 Perhaps the greatest mistake in the modern church is its unrecognized tendency to encourage Old Way living. Books, sermons, and seminars present an appealing blessing, then tell us how to get it. "God longs to bless you," we hear. "Live in such a way that His blessings are released into your lives." 📖

Have you seen this tendency for yourself in contemporary Christianity? If so, what examples can you cite?

> 📖 We're living under deception. The supreme blessing He longs to give us is Himself. No other blessing is guaranteed until heaven. The blessings we now claim are so often something less than an empowering, enlivening, pride-destroying, self-effacing, joy-giving encounter with God. 📖

14. How do you respond to Dr. Crabb's statement in the preceding quotation?

15. "This widespread deception," Dr. Crabb notes, "has consequences."

> 📖 1. *It breeds confusion and pressure.* Wasn't I a good enough husband? Is that why she left me? I tried so hard to be a good parent. What did I do wrong? Was I too firm? Not firm enough? What do I do to make things better? God, why won't You tell me what I can do that will work?...
>
> 2. *It weakens our view of God.* If the Christian life is all about blessings, then when trials come instead, we conclude either that we aren't living right or that God isn't really in control. In *this* situation, at least, Satan must enjoy the upper hand....
>
> 3. In the Old Way, *humility becomes a technique.* We humble ourselves and draw near to God in hopes that He'll draw near to us, not to let us *encounter* Him, but with *blessings* in hand. Humility becomes a maneuver. We come with empty hands but with a finger pointing: Give us that! Dependence gives way to methodology. 📖

In what ways, if any, have you experienced any of these consequences?

16. Another consequence, says Dr. Crabb is this one: *"We develop a wrong view of psychological problems."*

📖 I've been wondering: Could Old Way living have more to do with our troubles than we suspect? Does our insistence that this life provide more satisfaction than it can, and our determination to figure out some way to get it, lie beneath what we call psychological disorder? 📖

In pursuing this issue further, Dr. Crabb explores the first chapter of Paul's letter to the Romans:

📖 "Although they knew God," Paul said, people "neither glorified him as God nor gave thanks to him, but their thinking became futile.... Although they claimed to be wise, they became fools and exchanged the glory of the immortal God" for something else. "Therefore God *gave them over* in the sinful desires of their hearts to sexual impurity...to shameful lusts...to a depraved mind, to do what ought not to be done. They have become filled with every kind of wickedness, evil, greed and depravity" (Romans 1:21-29).

People pursue a source of primary satisfaction other than God. They do not value Him above all other treasures. That's the Old Way. Their thinking becomes futile. Their lives revolve around the false gods of better kids, good health, fulfilling relationships, effective ministries—anything other than God. And that devotion to a lesser god turns loose all manner of trouble. Selfishness rules. The springs of human nature are polluted. Vile water gushes out.

Like a shopper who mistakenly purchases the wrong size garment, we've exchanged the glory of God for an outfit we think might fit our soul a little better. We turn away from God and chase after other blessings. 📖

Summarize your understanding of the connection Dr. Crabb is making here between Paul's teaching in Romans 1 and the Old Way approach to living as described in this workbook.

17. Dr. Crabb notes three possible outcomes to our pursuing any primary satisfaction other than God:

📖 1. *We may experience enough blessings to persuade us we're on the right track.* Old Way thinking is confirmed as good. We're getting it right, and life is working. We become successful law keepers, modern Judaizers, happy Pharisees.

2. *A mixture of blessings and trials may keep us in the game and open us to any method to make life better.* We become pragmatists. Biblical principles are bent if we see personal advantage in compromise. Or we become legalists, more rigidly resolved than ever to do it right so life will work. We may decline into neuroticism, getting caught up in strange behaviors that protect us from internal pain.

3. *Life may become so hard, and our efforts to improve things may*

seem so futile, that we give up. Now we slide into major depression, conscienceless living, or insanity—serious neurosis, character disorder, or psychosis. 📖

In what ways have you observed any of these outcomes either in your life or in the lives of other Christians you know well?

18. Dr. Crabb continues exploring this issue in Scripture.

📖 With these thoughts in mind, I read another verse from Paul— and I tremble:

"The god of this world has blinded the minds of the unbelieving so that they might not see the light of the gospel of the glory of Christ, who is the image of God" (2 Corinthians 4:4, NASB).

Unbelievers do not see Christ as their greatest treasure. *Neither do most believers.* We live as blind people, chasing after the light we can see—the satisfaction that blessings bring—and not valuing the light we cannot see—the glory of Christ.

It could be different. We could live a new way. "For God, who said, 'Let light shine out of darkness,' made his light shine in our hearts to give us the light of the knowledge of the glory of God in the face of Christ" (2 Corinthians 4:6). 📖

What thoughts come to mind as you read these conclusions? In what ways is it easy for you to agree with them? In what ways do you find it difficult to agree?

19. Think about the most meaningful concept or truth you've explored in this week's lesson. How would you talk this over with God? Write your response here as a prayer to Him.

WHAT THE NEW WAY IS

*This week's lesson is based on
chapter 9, "Behind a Door Marked Private,"
chapter 10, "Coming Dirty and Dancing,"
and chapter 11, "Reaping What We Sow."*

At this point in *The Pressure's Off,* Dr. Crabb writes, "I dedicate the rest of this book to the growing number of people whose journey through life has been deeply disillusioning.... Whether through the emptiness of blessings or the anguish of trials, you're disillusioned."

📖 Your life isn't working, and you're losing hope that it ever will. You worry that your faith is weakening, that you're losing confidence in God....

Even when things go well, when wrongheaded faith and misplaced confidence seem validated, you sense an ache in your soul for something more. Your good marriage, good kids, good friends, good health, good church, good job, and good ministry don't satisfy. You receive whatever blessings come your way as mercies from God, and you're grateful. You do enjoy them—and you should.... But in the midst of enjoyed pleasure, you cannot suppress the question, "Is this all there is?" You're disillusioned by the emptiness of blessings....

The ache won't go away. Something is missing. But whatever it is, it's hard to find. The ache continues and deepens. Pornographic fantasies or expensive travel or rich desserts or frenetic ministry or hardened cynicism provide more relief than prayer. Or they provide no relief, and you're just miserable.

You want a new way to live, but you're not sure what it is, and you're not sure how to live it. 📖

1. In what ways, if any, does that description reflect your own experiences, past or present?

2. Listen with your heart to Dr. Crabb's invitation:

> 📖 I invite you to join me as I journey with you through a profoundly disillusioning life, a life filled with opportunities for shallow and temporary pleasure and fraught with unpredictable experiences of deep and lasting sorrow. Walk with me through the grocery store of existence on this planet, and notice that there are only a few stale donuts on the shelves.
>
> But let's keep our heads up and our eyes forward. I can see that door marked Private. Beneath that forbidding word I can make out the fine print: *Family Only Beyond This Point.*
>
> Let's remember that the blood of Jesus has opened a new way, a

living way—not into a method for making life work, but into the presence of God (see Hebrews 10:19-23). Let's not forget that Christ died for sin not to make our existence here pleasant, but rather to bring us to God, and that if we draw near to Him, He will draw near to us (see 1 Peter 3:18; John 14:21,23; James 4:8). 📖

What appeals to you most in this invitation?

To See and Savor Jesus

📖 Christians come in two varieties: those who trust Jesus to get them to heaven while trusting Him now to provide a good life of blessings till they get there, and those who trust Jesus to get them to heaven and discover that what they really want even now is to "see and savor Jesus Christ" [a phrase from author John Piper]. They're actually willing to lose every blessing and suffer any indignity if it will bring them into deeper relationship with Jesus. 📖

3. At this point in your life, how would you describe your desire for a deeper relationship with Jesus?

📖 This second variety of Christians—they're the New Way revolutionaries—have been disillusioned by the Old Way approach to life. Unexpected troubles, ones that cannot be traced to a specific failure on their part, have shattered their dreams of how their Christian lives would turn out. Senseless suffering, the kind they have no guarantee of avoiding in the future, has confronted them with a choice between two responses:

1. *Abandon God.* What good is He when life falls apart? It was His job to see to it that it didn't. He failed. He's a grocery store with empty shelves, holding no appeal to a starving man. If He doesn't stock what we need, or if we lack the money to meet His price for what is available, why bother with Him? To someone whose job was just lost, who cries every night from unrelieved loneliness, whose most important dreams have been shattered, a God who declares His benevolence is worth nothing.

2. *Abandon yourself to God,* humbling yourself enough to stop telling Him what He should be doing in your life, committing yourself to whatever He's doing, and believing it is good. 📖

4. Especially as you recall the most difficult troubles you've experienced in life, how difficult do you find it to follow the second response mentioned in the preceding quotation?

ONE SUPREME PASSION

In the New Way, Dr. Crabb writes, "we come to Him *as we are,* with full self-disclosure."

📖 Although we feel no pressure to be better or different, we intensely desire personal holiness more than we want relief from personal pain, and we're broken by how far short we fall. Tears over our self-centeredness and arrogance burn hotter in our eyes than tears over trials.

We come humbly, gratefully, and boldly, trusting that because of the Cross, God will come near, not to destroy us, but to embrace us, change us (sometimes painfully), and use us for His purposes. We keep coming and trusting, even when we see not a shred of evidence that He's warmly moving toward us or that we're meaningfully increasing in holiness. To keep coming toward the Light when all we can see is darkness is a measure of our absolute dependence. We have no other direction to go. 📖

5. In order to come to God fully in the way described in the preceding quotation, what kind of view of God should we have? What must we believe about Him?

📖 Whether we travel the Old Way or the New, there's a certain passion that fuels our movement along the path. Consider with me what that passion is. If we explore the depths of our hearts, and if we close our eyes to everything else long enough, we'll discover a core motive, a supreme desire, a compelling urge around which our entire lives revolve. Whatever we want *most* becomes the center of our lives. Like tribesmen dancing around a totem pole, our movements are all oriented around the object of our longing.

Call it our *first thing* passion. It isn't the only passion in our lives, but when a choice must be made, we dance around the thing that attracts us most. We're all loyal worshipers of something. 📖

6. As you think back, what have been your "first thing passions" at different seasons in your life?

📖 God asks only one question: "Am I your supreme passion or is it something else?" 📖

7. At this time in your life, is God your supreme passion, or is it something else?

📖 In the Old Way the passion that rules comes in a thousand varieties, but it consistently aims toward its central value—a *better life now!* Something must come to pass—some emotion must be felt, some increase in our sense of personal worth must be experienced, some thrill must delight us, some blessing must be granted—before life is worth living. As one woman put it to me after I preached on this subject, "Why would I come to God if He didn't give me what I wanted?" She hadn't yet realized that what her heart most deeply wanted was actually God Himself—and that's what He longs to give her. 📖

8. How would you answer the woman's question in the preceding quotation?

DANCING TOWARD THE THRONE

📖 We may want God, but experiencing God is not a predictable reality. We can arrange conditions favorable to encountering God, but we aren't in charge of whether He shows up.

Followers of the New Way realize they're mere beginners in the School of Divine Delights.

New Way revolutionaries accept their place in kindergarten; they realize they don't know much, but they're hungry to learn. And they're focused. They know what they're after. 📖

9. What is it that you most want to learn at this time in your life?

📖 It sounds extreme, perhaps unrealistic, but followers of the New Way want to know God more than they want anything else. Delightful children who love them; close friends they can trust; honor for what they do; success in family, job, and ministry; an experience of adventure and wonder as they live their lives—all desires, but all *second thing* passions. No blessing matters more to these people than the Blessing of Encounter. 📖

10. How "extreme" and "unrealistic" does the preceding quotation sound to you?

📖 For followers of the New Way, the Spirit's nudgings become recognizable. His wind fills their sails. They discover their center; they embrace their identity as spiritual, Spirit-ruled people; they cease defining themselves by their reflection in the thousand mirrors of others' expectations.

When they speak, they hear themselves as sheep bleating. Only then can they make out the Shepherd's voice. 📖

11. What does it mean personally to you to embrace your identity as a spiritual, Spirit-ruled person? In your own words, express this as fully as you can.

📖 Followers of the New Way dance with Christ to the rhythm of the Spirit into the presence of God. But they don't dance especially well. Sometimes they trip over their own feet. Sometimes they lose step with the rhythm and trounce on the Lord's toes....

Over time, after embarrassingly clumsy attempts, they begin moving to the Spirit's rhythm. They feel His nudge the way a woman feels her dance partner lead. They fix their eyes on Christ just as the dancing woman adoringly looks up to the one she trusts to set the pace. And they find themselves dancing toward a throne filled by the glory of sheer love. The Spirit blows them to their knees. The Son walks up the steps and stands by the throne, on the right-hand side. The Father speaks, "Welcome into My presence...." Joy! Joy! Joy! Peace! Love! Inexpressible joy! An encounter with God! A taste of what's to come. A taste never enjoyed by followers of the Old Way. 📖

12. What images in the preceding quotation match most closely your own longings for your relationship with God?

RADICAL GRACE

"The Old Way misses out on the chief blessing of seeing God," writes Dr. Crabb. "It requires that we pretend. We wipe our own noses, wash our faces, and sew the rip in our clothes—we make ourselves presentable. Then we say to God, 'Look what I've done. I got it right. My nose is clean. Now give me the blessings I want.'"

The New Way is in stark contrast:

> 📖 New Way revolutionaries believe in radical grace. They know there's no other way to become holy than first by being declared holy, then by wanting to be holy, and eventually by actually becoming holy.
>
> So they come as they are—insolent, filthy, whimpering, demanding—but they come. How else can they come? That's who they know themselves to be. But they come humbly. They know they're not attractive. They want God—He is their supreme desire, their first thing passion; they depend on grace—it's their only hope. It's our only hope. It's enough. So we come.
>
> And God draws near—in His timing, never in automatic response to our request. But He comes.... We realize that our nose is dripping, our face is dirty, and our clothes are torn. We don't yet see that Christ has already cleaned us up.... The Father looks at us, beaming with delight as if we were the most beautiful children in the universe.
>
> Then we realize: We're as beautiful to the Father as Christ is because we're *in Him!* The Father sings. And we collapse with gratitude at His feet. Filled with joy. The Son touches us on the shoulder. We stand. 📖

13. What does "radical grace" mean to you, how strongly do you believe in it, and how have you demonstrated that belief?

ALWAYS NUDGING

📖 Let me share two lessons I'm learning....

The first is this:

The Spirit of Christ is always nudging us toward the New Way if we're not on it and always nudging us farther along if we are. In every circumstance, at every moment, He's stirring our affection for God until He makes it the strongest passion in our hearts....

The Spirit is constantly nudging us toward the New Way and away from the Old, toward the Better Hope and away from demanding the Better Life. This first lesson I'm learning includes a radical and wonderful truth: *Pursuing my deepest pleasure and moving in rhythm with the Spirit both take me in the same direction—toward Christ!* Self-interest and worship go together if worship comes first. 📖

14. What is your reaction at this time to the concept that "self-interest and worship go together," as mentioned in the above quotation? Do you fully "buy in" to this? Do you have doubts or some other form of resistance to it?

If that concept is true, what difference should it make in your life?

15. Here's the second lesson Dr. Crabb says he's learning:

> 📖 *My passion to know Christ often seems weaker than my desire for blessings.* And unless this changes, I will not consistently live the New Way. I must therefore give disciplined thought to how my desire for Christ can be nourished.
>
> I tend toward superficial living. If life presents only a few bumps, especially if they're small, I don't particularly care whether I know Christ well or not. I figure He's doing His job of blessing me and I'm doing my job of living responsibly. Rather than a thirsty deer panting after water, I'm more like a hibernating bear with paws resting on my full stomach. 📖

In what ways can you identify with this description?

A LINEARITY STILL IN EFFECT

📖 Earlier…I suggested that the Old Way formula of linearity has been abolished. No longer can we work hard to get it right and claim a guarantee that life therefore will work. The Judaizers were dead wrong. The Law of Linearity, which they depended on, is not in effect.

But another linear relationship still holds. And when we see what it is, we'll be deeply interested in nourishing the appetite that will sustain us in New Way living.

Listen to the apostle Paul: "The one who sows to please his sinful nature, from that nature will reap destruction; the one who sows to please the Spirit, from the Spirit will reap eternal life" (Galatians 6:8).

That linearity is still in effect. We reap what we sow. 📖

16. In practical, everyday terms for your life at this time, what do you think it means to "sow to please the Spirit"?

17. "But notice," Dr. Crabb continues, "it isn't the linearity assumed by the Old Way."

📖 The promise of a cause-effect relationship between *getting it right* and *a life that works* is gone. God has put into effect a new linear arrangement:

If we choose the Old Way, we'll end up miserable. We may feel quite good for a long time, but every follower of the Old Way will end up feeling miserable.

GUARANTEED!

If we choose the New Way, we'll experience joy, perhaps after a long season of suffering and searching. But we'll find ourselves and be full, alive, happy.

GUARANTEED!

Choosing the New Way matters. Once you're saved, there's no more important choice. 📖

How do these "guarantee" statements compare with what you've previously thought about God's promises and the right way to live the Christian life?

18. What have you enjoyed learning and exploring most in this week's lesson?

THE IMMANUEL AGENDA

*This week's lesson is based on
chapter 12, "The Immanuel Agenda,"
chapter 13, "The Barn Door's Open,"
and chapter 14, "Story of God."*

Dr. Crabb portrays God's "Immanuel Agenda" as "the relentless obsession He has for forming a family to gather at His dinner table, with Himself at the head and each of us thrilled to be there."

Listen to the author's paraphrase and commentary based on John the Apostle's words in Revelation 21:2-4:

 "He is here…and He has not disappeared. God has let me see all that's happening from heaven's point of view. It's breathtaking. The Lamb is roaring His way through history to complete the Immanuel Agenda.

"I saw the Holy City, the New Jerusalem, coming down from heaven. It's coming down to us, to you and me. And as I watched, I heard a loud voice declare: 'Now the dwelling of God is with men, and He will live with them. They will be His people, and God Himself will be with them and be their God.'"

I hear John saying, "That's why God sent Jesus. It's the Immanuel Agenda: *God will be with us!* When that happens, when the Better Hope of drawing near to God is fully realized, we'll want nothing more. And that's when the Better Life will be ours as well. No more shattered dreams. Blessings beyond our wildest imagination. No reason to cry, ever, not even to sigh. And all of that with Jesus at the center.

"Stay the course, weary pilgrims. Don't lose heart. The Immanuel Agenda is about to be completed." 📖

1. What is most encouraging to you in that message from John?

Do you have any objections or doubts or qualms about this message? If so, what are they?

2. The author also imagines these words from John:

📖 "My little children, if you could see the Better Hope ahead, you would not require the Better Life now. He who was seated on the throne said—with my own ears I heard Him—'I am making everything new.' Then He looked straight at me and told me: 'Write this down, for these words are trustworthy and true. My people need to hear them.' I've written Revelation so you would never, no matter how difficult your life may become, lose confidence in Jesus" (Revelation 21:5, the author's paraphrase). 📖

What is most likely to tempt you to "lose confidence in Jesus"?

📖 Paul said much the same thing to people who thought the journey to heaven should include a few more blessings. "If only for this life we have hope in Christ, we are to be pitied more than all men" (1 Corinthians 15:19). 📖

3. What's the reason behind that statement of Paul's from 1 Corinthians 15:19? Why would that be true?

THE WIND OF THE SPIRIT

Into each of our lives, Dr. Crabb writes, "the wind of the Spirit is blowing."

📖 But it isn't moving our ship toward the smooth seas of a more pleasant life. It's rather carrying us into the eye of the storm, into the presence of God. And we must adjust our sails accordingly. If we aim for calm waters, we go alone. We resist the wind of the Spirit. 📖

4. What convinces you that the wind of the Spirit is blowing in your life?

    📖 The apostle John invites us…not into the satisfaction and pleasures of improved circumstances, closer relationships, and happier feelings, but into the inexpressible joy of drawing near to God.

    Listen to him speak about it:

    "We have heard! We have seen! Our hands have touched! *Life has appeared!* And we proclaim it to you. We can now have fellowship with God. Our fellowship is with the Eternal Father of Endless Love and with His Magnificent Son, the One who died for us, Jesus Christ. We can draw near to God. I know the joy of coming into His presence. I want you to know that joy as well. Then my joy will be complete" (1 John 1:1-4, author's paraphrase). 📖

5. What does "fellowship with God" mean to you—and what do you most *want* it to mean in your own experience?

6. In the following quotation, Dr. Crabb encapsulates the core messages of John's gospel, of the book of Revelation (the "unveiling" to John), and of John's epistles:

📖 In his gospel John tells us, "You can trust Christ. He is who He says He is. Life is knowing Him."

In the unveiling…he says, "You'll stay the course through any storm if you know what's coming. And right now, when everything goes against you, the Lamb of the Cross is the Lion of Heaven moving toward His sure purpose. And it's a *good* one. Hang on!"

In his epistles, John issues an invitation: "In the middle of a difficult life, draw near to Jesus. It's the source of your deepest joy."

In everything he wrote, John is presenting the Immanuel Agenda. From the beginning of time, God has determined to be with us. *He will be our God,* as we value no treasure more than knowing Him, and *we will be His people,* gladly clinging to Him in worship and absolute dependence no matter what happens in this life. 📖

How do these core messages relate to your own desires to turn from the Old Way and live fully in the New Way of the Spirit?

7. "The agenda," says Dr. Crabb, "is on track."

📖 God is with us now. He's here. Not the way He'll be here when the Holy City comes down, but He's here to be enjoyed. Our highest calling, our deepest joy, is to celebrate His availability by drawing near to Him, not to use Him to make our lives better, but to enjoy Him for who He is.

It's a different understanding of the spiritual journey. John invites his readers to walk a new path, to live a new way. We're asked to experience without complaint the disadvantages of a difficult life in order to more deeply experience the "precious thing" of communion with God. 📖

In what ways for you is this indeed "a different understanding of the spiritual journey"?

RICH TOWARD GOD

📖 Someone in the congregation came to me after I preached and said, "Am I hearing you right? Surely you aren't saying that we come to God only to know Him. Unless He gives me the blessings I need to be happy, I can't see why I'd come to Him at all. Your teaching makes me want to not even bother with God."

I mentioned this woman in an earlier chapter. I think she's related (as all of us are) to a man who once called out to Jesus while He was teaching. 📖

Dr. Crabb unfolds this story from Luke 12:13-21.

> 📖 "Someone in the crowd said to him, 'Teacher, tell my brother to divide the inheritance with me.'"
>
> He wanted a better life of more money. Likely it was his due. Fairness was probably on his side. Notice the Lord doesn't even enter the "who's right" debate, something I often do when I listen to one spouse tell me how wrong the other one is.
>
> "Jesus replied, 'Man, who appointed me a judge or an arbiter between you?'" 📖

8. Why do you think Jesus responded to the man's request in this way? (After all, as Dr. Crabb comments, "I thought Christ *was* the judge. Who could be more qualified? Jesus would know the heart of both brothers, and He would know what was right.")

> 📖 "Then he said to them [to the whole crowd, leaving the bitter man still indignant over his plight], 'Watch out! Be on your guard against all kinds of greed; a man's life does not consist in the abundance of his possessions.'"
>
> He sidestepped the fairness issue completely. It wasn't His concern. It would be difficult to imagine a clearer warning against living the Old Way: *Don't make it your goal to get out of life what you want.* He called it greed. It's the foundation of Old Way living. 📖

9. How would you define *greed* in its widest biblical meaning and as it relates to your everyday life?

📖 To drive home His point, He did what He often did. He offered a story.

"And he told them this parable: 'The ground of a certain rich man produced a good crop.'"

Some people are blessed. I know godly men and women who are rich. I know godly men and women with effective, far-reaching, and much-honored ministries. Blessings are good. We're to enjoy them and use them well. But blessings are dangerous.

"'He thought to himself, "What shall I do? I have no place to store my crops."'" He doesn't even mention God. All that's on his mind is to enjoy his good fortune and to keep it coming. When your goal is a better life, you're completely selfish. 📖

10. If blessings are genuinely good, why are they also dangerous?

In what ways do you agree or disagree with Dr. Crabb's conclusion in the preceding quotation—"When your goal is a better life, you're completely selfish"?

11. Jesus continues the parable:

> 📖 " 'Then he said, "This is what I'll do. I will tear down my barns and build bigger ones, and there I will store all my grain and my goods. And I'll say to myself, 'You have plenty of good things laid up for many years. Take life easy; eat, drink, and be merry!' " ' "

He had worked hard, and it paid off. *A* led to *B*. And he liked it. The Old Way is deeply satisfying—not, however, in the deepest depths and not for long.

" 'But God said to him, "You fool!" ' " Today, we'd expect congratulations. "Way to go" seems more appropriate. We've worked hard, we've been diligent in wealth management, and now we can enjoy the Better Life of Blessings. We honor people, including ourselves, whose priority is achievement and who have succeeded. God called this one a fool, and said, " 'This very night your life will be demanded from you. Then who will get what you have prepared for yourself.' This is how it will be," Jesus promised, "with anyone who stores up things for himself but is not rich toward God." 📖

What do you think it means in your life right now to be "rich toward God"?

📖 Jesus went on to warn us about worrying over our lives down here, what we will eat, how our bodies are doing, whether we'll be able to provide for ourselves what we need. He finished this thought by telling us that our hearts belong to what we treasure most. (Luke 12:34—"For where your treasure is, there your heart will be also.") 📖

12. Where is your "treasure" now? To what "treasure" does your heart belong?

DRAWING NEAR

13. Think about the following words from God's point of view rather than your own:

📖 We must realize what God is doing whenever He withholds blessings we legitimately desire: He is pursuing the Immanuel Agenda. *He will be with a people who value Him above every other blessing.* He will create that people at the cost of His Son's death and at the cost of being hurt every day by children who really don't want Him except to use Him. He is allowing good dreams to shatter to arouse the better dream of knowing Him. 📖

What impressions of God's character do you gain from those words?

BELIEVE AND WATER FLOWS

Dr. Crabb says that the New Way begins with this promise: "Water is available, and you may drink it, but life may be tough as you draw near."

📖 The focus of the New Way, however, is not on the trials; it's on the availability of cool water and rich food.

"Whoever believes in me...streams of living water will flow from within him" (John 7:38).

That's New Way linearity: Believe and water flows.

"Come, all you who are thirsty, come to the waters.... Eat what is good, and your soul will delight in the richest of fare" (Isaiah 55:1-2).

More New Way linearity. It's a promise! Come along the path God has opened through Christ into His presence—and you'll be satisfied!

"Give ear and come to me; hear me, that your soul may live. I will make an everlasting covenant with you" (55:3).

That's the arrangement. It's a good one. If we hear what He offers, we'll not want to change a thing. 📖

14. Do you "hear what He offers"? Express here, in the most meaningful way for you, your understanding of what God is offering you.

Now add your prayerful response to this offer.

How to Live the New Way

*This week's lesson is based on
chapter 15, "Enjoying God,"
and chapter 16, "Five Building Blocks
of New Way Living."*

"Perhaps the Spirit is stirring you as He is me," writes Dr. Crabb. "I long to live the New Way. If there's a road that leads to whatever enjoyment of God is available in this life, I want to take it.

"My prayer is that you do as well. I trust this book so far has aroused your desire to leave behind the pressure of arranging for your own satisfaction and to live in the freedom of knowing God. If it's possible to actually meet God in joy-producing encounter (and even partial joy in meeting God is inexpressible), then you want to walk whatever path leads into His presence. That's my prayer for you and for me as well....

"Now that we're willing, how do we live in the Spirit's New Way? That's the question I discuss in the remaining chapters of this book.

"The pressure's off!

"It's time to experience our freedom."

ENJOY THE FEAST

📖 If you believe it's possible to enjoy God and if you're becoming aware of your desire to actually meet Him, then you've come to a fork in the road. The Old Way—trying hard to do things right so the good things of life come to you—is still available. The allure is powerful....

But you see another path. The sign marking its entrance is shaped like a cross, and the words on the crossbeam read "The New Way of the Spirit." You have a choice to make. 📖

1. At this point in your life, how strongly do you feel drawn to the Old Way? How powerful for you is its allure?

📖 The phrase *image of God* begins to mean something. You realize that your identity, your joy, and your purpose are completely wrapped up in your relationship to God. He is the source, the only source, the complete source, of everything you were built to enjoy. More money, great marriage, beautiful kids, close friends, good ministry—nothing else does it. Perhaps you've tried a few out-of-bounds pleasures. They worked well, but only for a moment. Then deeper emptiness. More addictions. You began to realize you'd been sold a false bill of goods. Lies, all lies....

Blessings are good, but they're not enough. Not for your soul. And now you know you have a soul. You *are* soul, created by God for God to find yourself in God and then to live your life through God.

You cannot rest until you rest in God. You cannot celebrate as you were meant to celebrate until you celebrate God more than everything else that is good—or bad. 📖

2. As honestly as you can, describe your own journey in encountering any of the observations and experiences presented in the preceding quotation.

3. Consider carefully these points:

📖 It's time to shed our cynicism, to move beyond nonsacrificial living, and to abandon everything getting in the way of a deep experience of God. I hope you're desperate for a divine encounter, a genuine, noncontrived, deeply felt meeting with God that *both* exposes sinful pleasures as cheap counterfeits of soul joy *and* reveals to us that our nervousness about whether our lives will turn out well is an insult to the God who gives you Himself and says, "Enjoy the feast!"

Of course we'll continue to hurt when bad things happen. *Hurt* over trials, like pain from a kidney stone, is human, not sinful. But *despair* is sinful. It's subhuman to feel as if your source of real joy has been taken from you when a child rebels or a loved one dies or a business fails or an immoral temptation wins.

God is still present....

A former mentor, now partying in heaven with full enjoyment of God, told me, "The Christian always has reason to celebrate. When we fail, celebrate His grace. When we are blessed, celebrate His mercy. When others reject us, celebrate His love." 📖

At this point in your life—this very day—what does it mean for you to "shed your cynicism"?

What does it mean for you—today—to "abandon everything getting in the way of a deep experience of God"?

Today, what do you have to celebrate, and why?

Relating with Others

As you discover your appetite for God, you may also be discovering your secondary appetite for relationship with others. You long for conversations that matter. At some point, you'll realize how strongly you want to bless others even if you're not blessed by others. If you're where I am on the journey, you're more aware of wanting to relate in ways that will lift you to a higher level of spiritual experience.

You long to be involved in a few relationships where you can be *known* in loving safety, *explored* with genuine interest, *discovered* by hopeful wisdom, and *touched* from the source of spiritual power.

4. As you think about the perspectives in the preceding quotation, how would you express your own deepest longings for your relationships with others?

The idea of a New Way sounds faddish, like a well-marketed overstatement. Even biblical discussion of this New Way, what you've read so far in this book, can seem like cotton-candy theology. Although the phrase "the new way of the Spirit" was inspired by the Spirit and written by the apostle Paul, it can come across as a lot of fluff and sweetness that offers nothing to sink your teeth into as you live in this world.

5. Have you had similar thoughts to those Dr. Crabb just described?

🕮 The phone rings. Something has gone wrong, and you must deal with it. At that moment, talk of enjoying God sounds like an annoying platitude, a pious irrelevance, something of interest only to monastics, contemplatives, people so right-brained that they're out of touch with real-life challenges, people so mystical that they're more interested in spiritually retreating than facing life.

You've got a problem on your hands, a fire to put out. You're wide open to help from God—but *enjoying* Him?…

Enjoy God? When your son's been arrested? When your marriage isn't working? When your wife comes down with Alzheimer's? When your loneliness reaches new depths you can no longer tolerate? When the sexual struggle you thought was under control comes back with more uncontrollable passion than ever?

Enjoy God? *In the middle of all that?* 🕮

6. Again, describe any ways in which your own reactions have been similar to those expressed by Dr. Crabb in the preceding paragraph.

7. Dr. Crabb responds, "Enjoy God? Yes. In the middle of hard times? *Especially* then."

   For your own life, how realistic and practical is this counsel from Dr. Crabb?

📖 In the New Way, whatever we do comes out of a heart that has already come to God, that is anchored in that relationship, that looks to God for whatever joy and hope is needed to carry on, that demands nothing but celebrates God in everything. In the New Way, truth is personalized. For New Way revolutionaries, to live is Christ—not raising godly kids or making new friends or even living morally. 📖

8. What does it mean for you that "truth is personalized"?

LET ISAAC BE BORN!

Dr. Crabb looks at Abraham's life to show us a meaningful picture of the Old Way versus the New.

📖 When God appeared to the patriarch and said, "You, my aged friend, and your elderly wife will have a baby in one year," Abraham was not excited. "God," he replied (the story is told in Genesis 17), "I've heard that before. Years ago, You told me that Sarah and I would bear a child. Well, it hasn't happened. And now it's too late. It would take a miracle for us to conceive now. I'm not sure I want to be stretched to that level of faith. I've lived by faith in a lot of situations. I left my home on nothing more than Your word. But now You're pushing it. I'm a little tired of living by faith. Frankly, God, I've about given up hope. I think I'd prefer a manageable life, a natural one." 📖

9. To what extent can you identify in your spiritual life with such a response from Abraham? Are you ever "tired of living by faith"?

📖 Then Abraham looked across the plains toward his tent. There sat his once beautiful wife, now a ninety-year-old woman, sexually uninviting, sexually inadequate, and probably sexually disinterested. Ishmael, his teenage son by another woman, was there too. A fine, healthy young man.

Abraham had an idea. "God, how about if You provide me Your promised blessings through the son I already have? Ishmael was born in the natural way, I grant that. No miracle was required, just a moment of compromise. That would make things so much easier. I already did something that worked. Couldn't you let that be enough? Oh God, *let Ishmael live!*" (See Genesis 17:18.)

That's been my cry for fifty years. I want to know that I can do something that will bring about the blessings I desire. To wait for a miracle puts me out of control. I don't like that. I want to believe that if I get it right, my life will work, that God will bless me with whatever I think I need in order to feel joy. "Please, God. You didn't do it for Abraham, but You had special plans for him. In my life, please, *let Ishmael live!*" 📖

10. In what way has your own heart's cry been, "Let Ishmael live"?

📖 To get started on the New Way, we must change our prayer. "God, I don't know how You can produce the fruit in my heart of a consuming love for You. I seem to find so much more enjoyment in the good things of life, and sometimes in sin, than in knowing You. I like blessings more than I love You. I experience more pleasure in other things than in You. It will take a miracle to change that.

"You tell me the miracle has already happened, that I have a new heart that wants You as my ultimate pleasure. But I don't know how to make that real. I can come to You as I am, like Abraham came to Sarah, as a tired old man. It took a miracle for them to conceive. But You did it. I will trust You for a similar miracle in my life. God, I now cast out Ishmael and his mother (see Galatians 4:21-31). I want no more temptation to return to the old way of making my life work. I want to lead a supernatural life. I come to You as I am. *God, let Isaac be born!*" 📖

11. In what ways does your heart cry out now, "God, let Isaac be born"?

RENEWING THE WAY WE THINK

📖 The revolution I envision will be fueled by the New Way to think, live, and relate. It begins with thinking. We're transformed by renewing our minds, not our circumstances; we're changed not by rearranging blessings in our lives or strategizing to make life work a little better or overcoming our low self-esteem and troubling emotions, but by renewing the way we think about this life. 📖

12. In what important ways do you see that your thinking has already been renewed through what you've explored and learned in this workbook?

TAKING A DEEPER LOOK

*This week's lesson is based on
chapter 17, "Where Am I? Finding the Red Dot,"
chapter 18, "Your Choice of Cycles,"
and chapter 19, "First Thing Focus."*

"I invite you now to join me," writes Dr. Crabb, "in taking a deeper look into our interior worlds. As we do so, keep in mind one vital truth that will sustain us: *Brokenness is the path to freedom.* When we see in ourselves things we wish were not there and realize we can do absolutely nothing to clean up the dirt we find, we enter into the liberating experience of brokenness.

"How long we stay there before we feel freedom is up to the Spirit. It may be days, weeks, years. Sometimes the fruit of our affliction is visible only in our legacy. We simply must trust the Spirit. Comfort is His sovereign work."

BROKENNESS

📖 God ordains afflictions and trouble (see Hebrews 12:5-6), but always for the purpose of setting us free to serve Him in the New

Way of the Spirit. That Spirit, on His timetable, shines the spotlight on grace and lets us feel Him pour the Father's love into our hearts no matter how we fail and struggle.

It's the taste of divine love, unlike any love we've known, that draws us to the table for more food. At times we can almost see the Spirit smile as He nudges us toward the table and pulls out our chair for us to sit.

Listen closely and you might hear Him say:

"You can come as you are, right now. No penance, just repentance. Yes, I know—you see the mess. I've helped you see it. But the Father sees only the beauty of Christ. Come! Eat. Drink. Enter His presence under the terms of the New Covenant. You are as pure as Christ. You belong to the Father. You desire Him above all other desires. And now I'll deepen your awareness of all that is true, freeing you to come boldly into a place where many have died. Come in the merits of the Cross." 📖

1. Which words and phrases in the preceding quotation can you indeed sense coming to you now from God's Spirit? What else do you sense the Spirit's saying to you?

📖 Brokenness and freedom go together, in that order; first suffering, then comfort; first trouble, then joy; first felt unworthiness, then felt love; first death to the self, then resurrection of the soul.

It's a cycle. First down, then up, then down again, farther down, then up again, this time higher. When we discover the red dot that marks where we are on our journey, we'll always experience brokenness. It's the continual starting point for every next step toward God. Brokenness helps us turn our eyes, not toward the blessings of a better life—those blessings never heal brokenness; they only cover it—but toward the intimacy promised as our better hope.

It is the failure to discover where we are at any moment that keeps us from realizing where we most want to go. Until we face an inner brokenness that no blessing in this life can mend, we'll be drawn irresistibly to the Old Way. 📖

2. What does *brokenness* mean to you?

📖 Now let's see how this works. The New Way journey begins with a stunning revelation, not about us, but about God. The unapproachably holy, incomparably magnificent God wants us to *enjoy* Him, to actually come close and feel really good. He made us for the pleasure *He* enjoys when *we* enjoy Him.

But He, quite properly, is a jealous God. For Him that's only reasonable. He demands we enjoy Him as our supreme good because that's what He is....

God will never allow us to fully enjoy Him as long as we think of Him as one good among many. For one simple reason: It can't be done....

When God's people declare loyalty to Him but demand pleasure elsewhere—spouse, children, friends, ministry, health, success—God charges them with adultery. That's a capital offense. So, first, God kills His Son in their place. Then, like Hosea with Gomer, He separates Himself from them, *but only* to win them back to enjoyed nearness. The separation is designed to arouse their appetite for what is missing, to heighten awareness that only God's presence can satisfy the depths of human desire. 📖

3. What is your understanding of exactly how and why God wants you to enjoy Him?

📖 Consider God's invitation to us....

As our Father, God welcomes His children to the family table and there spreads a magnificent feast—*Himself.* "Come, take your place secured by My Son. My Spirit has brought you here. Now, look at Christ to see Me. Drink Me. Eat Me. Satisfy yourself with My love that lets you see Me and live. Be awed by My splendor and majesty till you realize there is none brighter, none like Me, that you are fish and I am the ocean. All other water is but a puddle of mud in comparison." 📖

4. Record your response here to the words of invitation in the preceding quotation.

Where You Are

"The first step in our drawing near to God, to tasting any passion and vision for Him," writes Dr. Crabb, "is to identify where we are. If we draw near to Him, He *will* draw near to us. It's a promise. What more could we want?"

📖 Now we're ready to ask the question: *Where am I?*...

On the authority of God's Word, I can tell you where you are. It's where I am. I can tell you what's going on inside you. And if you see it, if you recognize where you are, you'll be drawn to the New Way. You'll abandon your love affair with blessings, and you'll bow low before God, demanding nothing. So will I.

There are two distinct attitudes within us. The first is in everyone, Christian or not. Isaiah looked at the people in his day and saw that all of them, like sheep, had gone a wrong way. Everyone had turned to the way that made natural sense: *Do whatever you think is best, and expect life to work.* Isaiah's diagnosis is severe: "From the sole of your foot to the top of your head there is no soundness— only wounds and welts and open sores" (Isaiah 1:6; see also Isaiah 53:6)....

That is the energy of the Old Way. I feel it moving in me. And I know that it's strong. I know it's so strong that only a direct encounter with God will stir the better energy in me until it rules my life. 📖

5. How have you most recently recognized within yourself the reality of this first attitude, this "energy of the Old Way"?

6. "The *second* attitude," writes Dr. Crabb, is "the better energy in every Christian's soul that too often lies unnoticed and unstirred."

📖 Can you feel…an energy moving you toward God, not to use Him, but to become absorbed with Him, to honor Him, at any cost? Is there an appeal to the prospect of simply presenting yourself, with all your disappointments, demands, and discouragements, to the Father, then remaining steadfast and faithful while you wait for Him to draw near to you? *God, I come to You. Let me know You. That's what I most want.* 📖

How have you most recently recognized within yourself the reality of this second attitude, the "energy moving you toward God"?

NARROW ROAD, NARROW DOOR

📖 What did Jesus have in mind when He said there's a way to the abundant life of knowing and enjoying God, but "small is the gate and narrow the road that leads to life, and only a few find it" (Matthew 7:14)?…

Make every effort, Jesus said, to find the narrow door leading to life because "many, I tell you, will try to enter and will not be able to" (Luke 13:24). 📖

7. How would you answer the opening question in the preceding quotation?

📖 Choosing the New Way is costly. If we don't regard God as our chief joy, we won't have the capital to pay the price. It's by faith we see Him as the source of supreme pleasure; it's a faith that keeps us coming to Him until He gives us a taste of the pleasure we believe is available, and then coming to Him again.

If we do regard God as our chief treasure and live accordingly, we'll seem inhuman to some; we'll appear as radical freaks who take God too seriously and end up leading an unbalanced life. 📖

8. To the best of your understanding, what do you see as your personal cost in choosing the New Way?

📖 Remember the proud Pharisee who came into the temple, stood up tall, and *prayed about himself?* "God, I thank you that I am not like other men—robbers, evildoers, adulterers—or even like this tax collector. I fast twice a week and give a tenth of all I get" (Luke 18:11-12).

In other words, I got it right. Now bless me!

Notice the difference between the proud Pharisee and the humble tax collector. Neither had any right to claim God's blessings. One knew it. The other didn't. The Pharisee still believed in the modified Law of Linearity: If we get the law mostly right, then everything we do will prosper. The tax collector pinned all his hopes on the Law of Liberty—come as you are, undeserving, broken, desperate, and trust God will come near to you rather than banish you from His presence—which is all you deserve.

A principle worth remembering emerges from this parable:

Self-discovery that is led by God's Spirit always generates brokenness, deepens humility, and energizes dependence and gratitude. 📖

9. With the words of the preceding quotation in mind, think about the following New Way attributes, and converse with God about them. Record in writing a summary or section of your prayer.

brokenness

humility

dependence

gratitude

TELLING CHARACTERISTICS

Dr. Crabb lists the following three characteristics of those "who never recognize the bad energy within them as bad, and who never gratefully delight in the new energy that is even more deeply lodged in their being."

📖 *Followers of the Old Way organize life into a System.*

They hate mystery, they do all they can to resolve tension, they work to find some way to bring into their lives whatever blessings they believe will make them happy. They love the idea of linearity; it sustains the illusion of control. Find the system that makes life work—find the *A* that leads to *B*. It prolongs the hope of a better life now. 📖

10. To what extent, if any, have you seen in your own life this linear system-organizing tendency as well as a disliking of mystery?

📖 *Followers of the Old Way deny whatever reality they come across that contradicts their System.*

When a tither goes broke, he finds a way to fault his tithing. As a child, I could never figure out why I sometimes aced a math test the day after I was bad. I explained it by assuming I had been good enough to offset the bad I had done. 📖

11. In what ways have you found yourself denying the reality of any evidence that contradicts your "system"?

📖 *Followers of the Old Way mistake vulnerability for brokenness.*

They're willing to "get real" and "tell it like it is," assuming that their vulnerability is a virtue deserving compassion. They become aware of their longings, perhaps even their thirst to know God better, but remain ignorant of either their thirst for God Himself or their falling short that disqualifies them from receiving any blessing apart from mercy. It is characteristic of the Old Way to become aware of only those longings that some blessing other than God's presence can satisfy. It sustains the pride of independence. 📖

12. In what ways does the description in the preceding quotation reflect your own approach to vulnerability, past or present?

Dr. Crabb then lists the three following characteristics of those "who recognize both energies within them, who discover the small gate, and who…step through it in brokenness to walk the narrow New Way."

📖 *Followers of the New Way accept the unresolvable tension in life.*

Mystery remains and always will. They realize no system can be known or harnessed that will make all of life predictable.... Although sometimes terrified, New Way followers step into the mystery of life with no final hope other than a gracious sovereign God, who moves in a mysterious way. 📖

13. How easy is it for you to accept life's unresolvable tensions?

📖 *Followers of the New Way struggle to be truly authentic.*

When life confuses or enrages them, they admit it. When God disappoints and frustrates them, they talk it over with Him—and others. They enter dark nights with trembling confidence that somewhere there is light and someday they'll see it. Their rest is in the present God. 📖

14. To what extent does the preceding quotation reflect your own attitudes?

📖 *Followers of the New Way are cautious about vulnerability but vulnerable to brokenness.*

They recognize that what we call vulnerability is often a narcissistic parade intended to draw support. These folks prefer to face in themselves only what draws them closer to God. Sharing pain is secondary. Sharing hunger for God and facing what impedes their search for Him is primary. Their excitement is in the relational God. 📖

15. How would you explain in your own words the approach to vulnerability mentioned in the preceding quotation?

Your Choice of Cycles

"If our foundation for thinking about life is the Old Way," Dr. Crabb writes, "if we believe that doing something right will make our lives work better, if we aim no higher than toward a better life, then we're likely to see only two paths open before us."

> 📖 I call the first the Adjustment Cycle. Here's how it works.
>
> Start by *denying* whatever you cannot handle.... Do whatever it takes to stay distant from difficult realities that might overwhelm your coping skills, whether that reality is inside your heart or outside in your circumstances.
>
> Then find your bootstraps, grab them, and pull up hard. *Strategize*. Life is hard. You admit that. But you can handle it. Let's see. How?...
>
> Now that you've experimented with several coping strategies, *evaluate*. See which ones seem to work best....

You are now ready to *refine* your approach to recovering your life....

There! You've got it now. You still have bad days, and nights are especially difficult, but you're getting through pretty well. Sometimes you feel really good.... The important thing is you feel restored. You like yourself. You like most of life. And you're able to keep your distance from the ache in your soul that tells you something is dreadfully wrong. The need to keep denying, strategizing, evaluating, and refining your methods continues. But for now you're pretty *stable*. The Old Way is working. Praise God! Or whomever. 🕮

16. In what ways have you seen yourself following this Adjustment Cycle?

🕮 Sometimes the Adjustment Cycle fails. You can't cope. When you're unable to develop a stable strategy for handling your life, the therapeutic culture offers its services. Consider the Therapeutic Cycle....

Start by lifting denial. *Openness* about how you "really feel" begins the cycle. Therapy creates a safe place for emotional vulnerability. Someone actually listens to you without disdain or judgment. And it helps. When you share your secret emotions and face the ones you've buried, you do feel better. The burden seems lighter. There! You're off to a good start. You feel hope.

Next comes *insight*. If your therapist is directive, the insight might be carefully presented. Otherwise, under the influence of probing questions, clarifying comments, and well-timed silence, you may come to new realizations on your own....

With insight comes *direction*. What course of action does your new awareness suggest?... Now you know what to do.... The energy of, well, *self* courses through your being. You feel strong, together, whole for the first time in your life.... You love your newly developing freedom.

But it's scary.... *Support* helps, from your therapist, from friends who love you and believe in you and take your side.... With help you can break out. You can do it!

Now comes the tough part. It's time to *align* your behavior with your insight, to move in the directions that now seem so right, and to do it with support. Remember Jesus loves you. He's *for* you. He wants you to love yourself and to feel the freedom to be who you are. Visualize Him cheering you on. Let Him, along with the Spirit, be your primary support group as you follow the Old Way to a better life. 📖

17. In what ways have you seen yourself following this Therapeutic Cycle?

📖 But there's a new way to live, and it's radically different. Be still. Reflect on where you are. You've been *using* God to make your life work. That puts you above Him. You're insisting that blessings come your way, at least certain ones. You're not *wanting* blessings; you're *requiring* them. You're depending on them for your joy. God is not your supreme treasure. Christ is not preeminent in your life. The Spirit lies quenched within you; His invitation to feast on God goes unheeded.

As you see what's been going on inside you…you feel more than a little sheepish. In your humility, you hear the Spirit whisper, "There's a new way to live. There's another path to follow." 📖

18. Be still and reflect on where you are. Have you been using God? Have you been requiring blessings instead of merely wanting them? Have you been depending on blessings for your joy? Is something less than God your supreme treasure? Respond to these questions here.

📖 New Life begins at the Cross. It's there you realize how arrogant you are. You don't welcome trials. You've lived for no greater purpose than to avoid them or reverse them if they come. Your ambition has risen no higher than a life that works pretty well…. God's glory has mattered little to you. A quality life is what you're after…. The Spiritual Cycle begins with *brokenness.* It hurts. The two Old Way cycles are much more seeker friendly. 📖

19. What does it mean for you at this time to come to the Cross?

📖 From brokenness the Spirit leads you to *repentance*. You've assumed you deserved satisfaction. You thought, with God's help, you could arrange for it. You believed you were living the Christian life. How could you have been so deceived? You thought God was here to cooperate with your agenda. But only He can say, "I AM." You can say only, "I serve at Your pleasure." 📖

20. What does genuine repentance mean for you at this time?

📖 Yes, this is a new way to think. Your mind has changed. Repentance has begun. And it feels clean, right, strangely good.

The Spirit then moves you from brokenness through repentance to *abandonment*.... You listen to the Spirit speak through the Bible. This world is fallen. Things happen that make no visible sense. But somehow, through it all, God is telling a good story. Without the ending, the story is not good. But nothing happens, nothing can happen, nothing ever will happen that God cannot redeem to move the story along to its glorious climax. You believe that. You therefore abandon yourself to the invisible God, the One who for a moment became fully visible as He hung on the cross. 📖

21. What does it mean for you at this time to abandon yourself to God?

📖 Abandonment, surprisingly perhaps, arouses *confidence*. The Spirit witnesses to your spirit that you do belong to God, that He is working all things together for good, that eternity will vindicate your choice to abandon the well-being of your soul to this mysterious, mostly invisible, seemingly fickle, certainly unpredictable God.... You know, because the Spirit tells you, that He is present as you walk the New Way toward the Better Hope of knowing, glorifying, enjoying, and revealing to others the wonderful, spectacular God who is really there. 📖

22. How confident are you in God at this time? How would you express in your own words the reason for this confidence?

📖 Spirit-given confidence that God is there and worthy of absolute trust breeds the freedom to *release* what is most alive within you. You begin to feel something stirring in your innermost being. It may take awhile, but at some point you realize, *These are the springs of living water!...* You find yourself released to be the person you've longed to be—loving, joyful, peaceful, patient, kind, gentle. Never perfectly, but sometimes at least genuinely. And now you praise God and no one else. 📖

23. Record here your prayer, in your own words, for God "to release what is most alive within you."

24. Think about the most meaningful concept or truth you've explored in this week's lesson. How would you talk this over with God? Write your response here as a prayer to Him.

COUNTING ON GOD

*This week's lesson is based on
chapter 20, "God Is in Control—of What?"
and chapter 21, "The Papa Prayer,"
plus the Epilogue, "With God in the Bathroom."*

"We live our lives on one of two foundations," writes Dr. Crabb.

"If we build on the first foundation, the flesh, our core passion will be for blessings, whichever ones we value most. And our core experience, beneath whatever else we feel, will be pressure, the pressure to live a certain way to get the life we want.

"If we build on the second foundation, the Spirit, our core passion will be for God, to know Him and honor Him in any circumstance. And our core experience will be freedom, the freedom to draw near to God across a bridge we neither constructed nor maintain. And in that freedom we'll discover both the passion to live well and the wisdom to know what that means."

GOD IS IN CONTROL—OF WHAT?

📖 God is in control. Of what? *Of seeing to it that nothing thwarts His plan for His people.* What is that plan? To give us a Better Life now, as we define it? No. It's to reveal Himself as the greatest treasure the human heart could ever imagine, to draw people into a relationship with Him that utterly delights their souls.…

God is in control of what He wants to accomplish. He's moving through all of history—through earthquakes and picnics, through terrorism and church dinners, through divorces and anniversary celebrations—toward one thing: the Immanuel Agenda. And He'll reach it. He'll have a people who think He is the greatest, who value knowing Him and worshiping Him and serving Him above all other blessings.…

I feel a great burden to be unmistakably clear: *We cannot count on God to protect us from suffering of any kind or measure. The worst evil can happen to the best Christian. But we can count on God to enable us to draw near to Him whatever happens and, eventually, to experience deep joy when we do.* 📖

1. At this moment in your life, what does it mean to "count on God" in this way?

THREE MIRACLES

"We can count on God," Dr. Crabb writes, "to perform three miracles in our lives."

📖 He wants to perform them, He can perform them, and He will perform them in the lives of New Way followers.… There's nothing we can do to make these miracles happen. By following the New Way, we create space for Him to work in a certain way. But we remain utterly dependent on His sovereign grace to bless us as He chooses and when He chooses. 📖

📖 Miracle 1: We'll encounter God.

We can come into God's presence as we are—lustful, envious, discouraged, ugly enough to be reviled, selfish enough to deserve rejection, arrogant enough to be stomped on—and be welcomed and enjoyed.

As we sense God's welcome and feel His delight, as grace stirs us, we discover that beneath all the stain and smell, we're actually beautiful, even desirable. We share in Christ's loveliness. We're pure, we belong at the Father's table, we like to be good, and the power to do good is in us. 📖

2. Express here, in honest words addressed to God, your trust and confidence that He will perform this first miracle in your life. Express also what this means to you.

📖 Miracle 2: We'll experience community.

With at least one other person, sometimes a handful, we'll enter into levels of closeness that surface enough conflict to sink any relationship—and spiritual intimacy will emerge. After feeling the impact of failure and hurt and reeling with defensiveness, recrimination, and withdrawal, we can expect, if we live the New Way, to discover a power within us sufficient to face every relationship-destroying force and to carry us into true community. 📖

3. Again, in honest words addressed to God, express your trust and confidence that He will perform this second miracle in your life and what it means to you.

📕 Miracle 3: We'll be transformed.

An encounter with God and an experience in community will open our eyes to see how unlike Jesus we really are. We'll be appalled. Like Job when he finally heard God speak, we'll acknowledge, "I am unworthy" (Job 40:4). And then, when we *see* God, we will, again like Job, exclaim, "My ears had heard of you but now my eyes have seen you. Therefore I despise myself and repent in dust and ashes" (42:5-6).

Brokenness and repentance will lead to abandonment. We'll never abandon ourselves to the Spirit as long as we think we can change without Him. But when we sense our desire not merely to feel good about ourselves and to enjoy life but to *resemble Jesus,* and when we realize how utterly incapable we are of moving even one step in that direction without supernatural help, we'll then abandon ourselves more fully to the Holy Spirit.

And then, at unplanned moments, we'll know living water is springing up within us. Something wonderful will come out of us, and we'll tremble with joy. When we stare into the chasm separating who we are from who we long to be and realize we have no means in our flesh to cross from one side to the other, and not until then, we will change. *The miracle of transformation will be humbly enjoyed.* 📕

4. Once more, express in honest words addressed to God your trust and confidence that He will perform this third miracle in your life and what this means to you.

ALL THE SPIRIT DOES

Dr. Crabb writes, "God has sent His Spirit to do a sevenfold work that makes it possible for us to live the New Way.... And the more we see all that He is doing, the more the pressure falls off.... Let me now describe that sevenfold work (I follow the outline provided by John Owens in his classic work *Communion with God*) and suggest how we can depend on all that the Spirit does as we seek to draw near to God."

5. The Spirit's first work is *reminding*.

> 📖 Just before He promised them peace, Jesus told His disciples that "the Counselor, the Holy Spirit, whom the Father will send in my name, will teach you all things and will remind you of everything I have said to you" (John 14:26).
>
> When dreams shatter, when terrorists win and marriages fail, the Spirit is not silent. He reminds us that what matters most is unthreatened. The Father's agenda is on track. Christ did all that was needed for us to draw near to God and for Him to draw near to us. And the Spirit will tell us that the Trinity can conceive no greater blessing.
>
> If we live the New Way, we'll spend time in Scripture, not to master content, but to hear the Spirit. And we'll sense a weighty

anchor holding our ship steady in the worst storm. Like a seasoned nurse coming to our bedside and saying, "I've just checked with the doctor. Your disease has been cured. You'll be fine," the Spirit reminds us what Jesus has said: "In this world you will have trouble. But take heart! I have overcome the world" (John 16:33). 📖

How do you see the Spirit doing this work in your life? Respond here as fully as you can.

6. The Spirit's second work is *glorifying.*

> 📖 When the Spirit comes, Jesus said, "He will bring glory to me by taking from what is mine and making it known to you" (John 16:14).
>
> Coming to God can seem so pointless....
>
> Coming to God may rouse hopes that might be dashed and often are.
>
> When I do come, I must come centrally to know Him, not to improve my life.... And when I do, the Spirit glorifies Christ by taking what belongs to Him—the eternal value of His life, death, and resurrection—and whispering to me, "The way is open. Whatever happens, God is in control of what matters most. Come boldly. Come close enough to hear the Father singing over you with delight."
>
> In whatever shape I find myself, in the midst of whatever I'm facing, I'll be accepted into God's presence, listened to, understood,

and given whatever my loving Father knows is best. Christ made that possible. To Him be the glory. That's what the Spirit is saying. It's His second work. 📖

Again, how do you see the Spirit doing this work in your life? Respond as fully as you can.

7. The Spirit's third work is *pouring*.

> 📖 The Spirit inspired the apostle Paul to say this: "God has poured out his love into our hearts by the Holy Spirit, whom he has given us" (Romans 5:5).
>
> It's so hard to believe we're loved. Not only do circumstances turn sour and God does nothing, but also we have never fully experienced from family or friends the kind of love we long to know. As in everything that matters most to our souls, we're utterly dependent on the Spirit to convince us that indeed we are fully loved and *can* rest in the love of God for us. He persuades us by pouring the Father's love into our hearts, which is a mystical process....
>
> When I meditate on the Cross, when I open myself to others' touching me with Christ's love by being broken before them, then I may experience the wholeness of being divinely loved. 📖

How is the Spirit pouring God's love into your life? In what ways do you see this?

8. The Spirit's fourth work is *assuring*.

📖 Are there more wonderful words for moral failures, lonely people, and abused victims to hear than "The Spirit himself testifies with our spirit that we are God's children" (Romans 8:16)?...

If we look only at our lives, we'll wonder if we're His. If we evaluate our progress along the spiritual journey, doubts will rise. But if we learn to listen to the Spirit, we'll *know* we are Christ's. And we'll delight in holy fellowship with God.... We *are* His children. 📖

In what ways has the Spirit given you assurance that you are God's child?

9. The Spirit's fifth work is *sealing*.

📖 When we came to Christ, not only were we included in Christ, but also, having believed, we were "marked in him with a seal, the promised Holy Spirit" (Ephesians 1:13).

Sealing means safety. The Spirit Himself is the seal. Sealed people are set apart from unsealed people. Think of it! You and I have been given into the keeping of the Spirit to guarantee our encounter with the Father and the Son. We're safe, not from bombs, cancer, or family heartache, but from even an inch of separation from the God who is in control of the Immanuel Agenda. We can come boldly into His presence. 📖

Express here your understanding of what the Spirit's sealing means to you.

10. The Spirit's sixth work is *anticipation.*

    📖 "Now it is God who makes both us and you stand firm in
Christ. He anointed us, set his seal of ownership on us, and put his
Spirit in our hearts as a deposit, guaranteeing what is to come"
(2 Corinthians 1:21-22).

    The Spirit is the *earnest* of our inheritance, the *deposit* of what's
ahead, and the *guarantee* that it's coming. He is a part of the whole,
a taste of the meal, a sample of what we can anticipate....

    God is essentially a community of passionate persons who pro-
foundly like each other. When He created people, He built into
them a capacity for that same kind of passion and enjoyment. And
when He redeemed us, He put within us one member of the Trinity
as a deposit, we might say a teaser, of what's coming. Given how
vividly the Bible speaks of the pleasure and satisfaction and joy that
God provides, we can only assume that the deposit within us is an
experienceable taste, a felt pleasure, a palpable emotion, a little sample
of what's in store for all of us. 📖

Because of the Spirit's work, what anticipation do you have?

11. The Spirit's seventh work is *anointing*.

> 📖 "But you have an anointing from the Holy One, and all of you know the truth.... The anointing you received from him remains in you, and you do not need anyone to teach you" (1 John 2:20,27)....
>
> Coming to God for the Better Hope of enjoyed intimacy with Him (which brings glory to His Name) releases something from us. Loving passion and discerning wisdom are given to us by the Spirit. We sense His leading on what to do. That's the anointing we have received from Him. It's a divinely directed game plan for dealing with whatever is going on in our lives....
>
> I take this seventh work of the Holy Spirit, this spiritual anointing, to mean that followers of the New Way will be given the passion and wisdom of Christ to respond to every challenge they meet in life. When the Spirit came on the incarnate Christ, He was granted wisdom, power, and delight-producing fear (see Isaiah 11:1-3). And now in Christ are hidden all the treasures of wisdom and knowledge (see Colossians 2:3). If we learn what it means to come to Him, we'll receive an anointing that enlightens us about what to do and empowers us to do it in any circumstance of life. 📖

What is your understanding and experience of the anointing you've received by God's Spirit?

THE PAPA PRAYER

"It has recently dawned on me," writes Dr. Crabb, "that there's an Old Way to pray and a New Way to pray."

> 📖 Old Way prayers come in at least three varieties:
>
> *Change that.* Whatever in my life is causing pain, I ask you to change it. Straighten out my daughter, give me a spouse, restore my health, provide an income.
>
> *Use this.* Show me what principles I'm to follow to make it happen. Direct me to the person or resources I need to help make it happen.
>
> *Satisfy me.* I long to feel alive, content, fulfilled, and happy. Do whatever it takes to make me feel satisfied with me, with life, and with You.
>
> Nothing is wrong with these prayers *unless they represent the deepest passion of our hearts.* Then they're Old Way prayers with more demands than petitions. 📖

12. In your own prayer life, how can you discern when those prayers—change that, use this, satisfy me—involve your deepest passions and become demands more than petitions?

Dr. Crabb writes, "We can pray a New Way...*Lord, I come.* That's the essence of the New Way prayer."

> 📖 I call it the Papa Prayer:
>
> *P*resent yourselves to God as you are.

*A*ttend to where you notice God's presence or absence.

*P*urge yourselves of whatever, at that moment, might be keeping you from noticing more of God.

*A*pproach God with abandonment and confidence, dedicating yourselves anew to coming to Him to know and enjoy and reveal Him, not to using Him to make your life better. 📖

13. The first part of the Papa Prayer is to *present yourself to God.*

📖 Reflect on your life. Be brutally honest, knowing by God's grace revealed in the New Covenant you'll discover nothing that will make God reject you and believing, because of that same grace, that beneath the dirtiest dirt lies radiant beauty.

What passions within you seem deepest? Ask a few (only a few) trusted friends for feedback: What are you like to be with? What's your "pull," that is, what do people sense you're wanting from them, what's your effect on them, in the moment?

Make the incredibly difficult decision to face yourself, to feel your rage, lust, and terror as well as your compassion, kindness, and joy. Pretend about nothing. But as you honor that commitment, avoid the twin errors of *denial* ("I'll face only what I can handle, what doesn't make me feel too threatened") and *obsession* ("I'll face everything all the time"). 📖

Exercise your soul at this time to present yourself to God as you are. Write here a record or summary of your prayer words at this time, in this first aspect of the Papa Prayer.

14. The next part of the Papa Prayer is to *attend to God.*

    📖 Where have you noticed God's *presence* in the past hour or day? Where have you been aware of a longing to sense that He was with you but felt only His *absence?*

    The spiritual journey is centered in the experience of God. But it's rooted in the revealed truth of God. Attend to what you experience of God, but during this part of the prayer, focus also on what you know is true, whether you experience it or not. Remember the sevenfold work of the Spirit as you ponder whatever biblical text you read.

    Listen to the Spirit remind you of all that Jesus said, especially that everything is under control. Nothing ever takes God by surprise. The Immanuel Agenda is on course.

    Hear Him glorify Christ. Everything you need to experience the life of true abundance is in Christ and in the New Covenant made in His blood.

    Notice when He pours love into your heart. Be still, tune your ear to the music of heaven, hear the Father sing over you with delight. 📖

Where have you noticed God's *presence* in the past hour or day?

Where have you been aware of a longing to sense that God was with you but felt only His *absence?*

Attending to God can continue in these ways:

📖 Depend on the Spirit's witness that you are a child of God, even when the evidence you see makes you wonder.

Relax in the safety of His seal on your life. No act of terrorism, no stock market slide, no medical scare, no rejection, no broken family has the power to thwart God's work in your life. Everything can be redeemed by the Spirit for good purposes.

Taste whatever sample He gives you of the meal that's coming. It might be a moment of overwhelming joy or a deep release of built-up pressure to get it right so God will bless.

Trust the Spirit's anointing. Anticipate that He'll grant you the passion and wisdom to handle every situation you face in a way that honors Christ and advances His agenda. 📖

Record here your further prayer experience at this time of attending to God.

15. The third part is to *purge yourself before God.*

📖 Start by reciting David's prayer: "Search me, O God, and know my heart; test me and know my anxious thoughts. See if there is any offensive way in me, and lead me in the way everlasting" (Psalm 139:23-24).

Reflect on what is in you—attitude, motive, determination—and on what you're doing that makes it difficult for you to hear the Spirit, to believe His Word, to trust God.

Assume whatever it is has roots in a preoccupation with yourself. A focus on *your* desire, *your* dreams, *your* hopes, *your* disappointments, *your* pain can drive you to Old Way living. The effect of a focus on self, though encouraged by the therapeutic culture and sanctioned by much Christian teaching, is to accept another gospel, the gospel that God is here for us more than we're here for Him. 📖

Record here a record or summary of your experience at this time in purging yourself before God.

16. The fourth part of the Papa Prayer is to *approach God because you want Him.*

📖 As you present yourself to God—with all of who you are, with all you know God to be, with all your ongoing struggle against the flesh—respond in faith to God's invitations:
  Come, all you who are weary.
  Come, all you who can't get it right.
  Come, all you who are struggling to make life work. 📖

What is your response to these invitations?

Approaching God can continue in these ways:

📖 You're aware of the burdensome pressure of Old Way living and the heinous arrogance beneath it, but you're also aware of a spiritual hunger, of a longing to come to God to...

glorify and enjoy Him in an *encounter* with Him,

join the *community* of His people,

be *transformed* by His Spirit till you actually resemble Jesus.

Expect to experience a sovereign joy that will displace every affection other than God from the center of your heart. Anticipate that, by the Spirit, the Father and Son will show themselves to you. Trust the Spirit to provide the loving passion and the spiritual wisdom you need to handle every situation in life in a way that furthers the Immanuel Agenda. 📖

Express here in prayer your desire for God, your hunger for Him.

📖 Tell God, with tears if they're there, with whatever genuineness is alive within you, that you want Him more than any other blessing— to know Him, adore Him, enjoy Him, serve Him, reveal Him, become like Him. As you pray, you'll find petition flowing from your heart for others, especially for their salvation and growth, and for yourself, that you'll be an instrument of grace. You'll come with confidence, making known all your burdens without a spirit of anxiety or demand, but with trust in a Father whose love can be trusted. 📖

What petitions are flowing from your heart at this time for yourself and for others?

With God in the Bathroom

📖 Permit a final illustration.

When I was three years old, our family lived for a while in my grandparents' big, old-fashioned house. The only bathroom was on the second floor.

One Saturday afternoon (I know it was Saturday—Dad was home), I decided I was a big boy and could use the bathroom without anyone's help. So I climbed the stairs, closed and locked the door behind me, and for the next few minutes felt very self-sufficient.

Then it was time to leave. I couldn't unlock the door. I tried with every ounce of my three-year-old strength, but I couldn't do it. I panicked. I felt again like a very little boy as the thought went through my head, "I might spend the rest of my life in this bathroom."

My parents—and likely the neighbors—heard my desperate scream. "Are you okay?" Mother shouted through the door she couldn't open from the outside. "Did you fall? Have you hit your head?"

"I can't unlock the door," I yelled. "Get me out of here!"

I wasn't aware of it right then, but Dad raced down the stairs, ran to the garage to find the ladder, hauled it off the hooks, and leaned it against the side of the house just beneath the bathroom window. With adult strength, he pried it open, then climbed into my prison, walked past me, and with that same strength, turned the lock and opened the door.

"Thanks, Dad," I said—and ran out to play.

That's how I thought the Christian life was supposed to work. When I get stuck in a tight place, I should do all I can to free myself. When I can't, I should pray. Then God shows up. He hears my cry—"Get me out of here. I want to play!"—and unlocks the door to the blessings I desire.

Sometimes He does. But now, no longer three years old and approaching sixty, I'm realizing the Christian life doesn't work that way. And I wonder, are any of us content with God? Do we even like Him when He doesn't open the door we most want opened— when a marriage doesn't heal, when rebellious kids still rebel, when friends betray, when financial reverses threaten our comfortable way of life, when the prospect of terrorism looms, when health worsens despite much prayer, when loneliness intensifies and depression deepens, when ministries die?

God has climbed through the small window into my dark room. But He doesn't walk by me to turn the lock that I couldn't budge. Instead, He sits down on the bathroom floor and says, "Come sit with me!" He seems to think that climbing into the room to be with me matters more than letting me out to play.

I don't always see it that way. "Get me out of here," I scream. "If You love me, *unlock the door!*"

Dear friend, the choice is ours. *Either* we can keep asking Him to give us what we think will make us happy—to escape our dark room and run to the playground of blessings—*or* we can accept His invitation to sit with Him, for now perhaps in darkness, and to seize the opportunity to know Him better and represent Him well in this difficult world.

Will we choose the Old Way, the way of pressure? "I'll do whatever You say; just get me out of here!"

Or will we discover both God's heart and ours and choose the New Way, the way of freedom and joy? "I'll sit with You anywhere, in darkness or light; just let me know You and serve You!"

It's time to choose the New Way of the Spirit and follow it until we play forever in the fields of heaven, always looking to Jesus as our greatest blessing.

It's time to be with God in the bathroom until He opens the door to eternity. *It's what we want.* 📖

17. To help you remember, summarize here the most valuable truths you've learned in going through *The Pressure's Off Workbook.*

IT'S TIME

📖 Let me end by paraphrasing the apostle James:

"Dear friends, when difficulties come, don't try to figure out what you can do to make things better. Welcome whatever is going wrong as a chance to more deeply encounter God, to enter community, and to experience transformation.

"If you're not sure how to actually do that, ask God, not for improved circumstances or happier experiences, but for the wisdom to let your suffering draw out your desire for God. When you ask for that, know that He gives generously and never criticizes you for where you are. Believe, don't doubt. If you waiver between wanting the New Way and still clinging to the Old, you'll receive nothing from the Lord.

"It's time, brothers and sisters, to abandon ourselves fully to God. There's a New Way to live. Draw near to God, and He'll draw near to you. He'll meet you, fill you, delight you, and use you to further the great plan of the ages, the Immanuel Agenda. Then we'll all go home" (see James 1:2-7; 4:8,10).

Are you weary?

Having trouble getting it right?

Struggling to make your life work?

The pressure's off.

There *is* a New Way to live. 📖

NIGHT QUESTION

"What am I doing wrong?" The question was never far from the woman's mind. To-night it screamed from deep places within her, demanding the answer that never came.

"Look at my life. Things aren't turning out as I'd hoped. Why don't I feel better about myself? Why is life sometimes so difficult? I must be doing something terribly wrong."

The woman did not believe she was being punished for wrongdoing by a vengeful deity, though that thought was sometimes hard to resist. She did, how-ever, believe there was a right way to live that would make her life work. Of course there was. But she could not find the way.

Here at home, at night, she couldn't pretend as easily as she did in her busy days that she was content, that God had blessed her enough for her to call Him good. In the aloneness that pressed against her soul, memories came back—of times when she'd felt alive and happy and good, and of times when she'd felt very bad.

Those memories often came to her, especially after evening descended, and they had shaped her vision of the better life she wanted, of the blessings she was willing to work for and therefore expected to come her way. The woman longed to feel again the joy she'd known earlier and to avoid the pain she could not forget. She knew what she wanted…but she couldn't find the way. Her life wasn't working.

"Thank You, God," the woman made herself pray as she crawled into bed. "I know You will take me to heaven when this life is over. Thank You for the gift of eternal life I could never work hard enough to earn. And I know You have a plan for me now, before I go home. I will continue to trust You to bring it about."

Before sleep came, she could hear herself add, "But what am I doing that's getting in the way? *What am I doing wrong?*"

In the bedroom's quiet darkness, the woman waited. Surely God would answer her question and show her what she must do to receive the blessings of a better life now, the blessings she was sure God intended His people to enjoy. "I'd do whatever it takes…if only I could know what it is." That was her last thought before sleep rescued her from the pressure to figure it out.

How much later it happened she never knew. The woman sat bolt upright in bed, wide awake, but in a different way than when her alarm clock sounded. This wide awake was wider. Had she looked now at that clock by her bed, she would have seen the digital display of four blinking zeros. She had entered a world beyond time.

The Voice had not awakened her, but she heard it clearly: "I've come to show you the New Way."

Who was there? Who had spoken? She could see no one. Had there been a body behind the Voice, she couldn't have seen it. The darkness was too thick.

"It's a dream," she said to herself. She would lie down again and let it pass.

The Voice spoke again in the same clear tone. "It's your time. I've come to show you the New Way. It's dark enough now for you to see."

This is no dream, the woman thought. "I'm glad you've come," she said aloud. "I desperately need to discover a new way. For a long time I've prayed to know how to make my life go better. Nothing I've tried so far has worked. I need to find the New Way you speak of."

"You're looking for another version of the Old Way. I've come to show you the New Way."

The woman was puzzled but not silenced. "I quite agree there are many ways that don't work. My life is proof enough of that. I've tried everything I can think of to change how I feel and to make my life go better. Please, if you have any mercy at all, show me what I'm doing wrong that's keeping me from what I so badly want. I'm eager to learn a new way. You'll find me a willing pupil."

"You're looking for a method to make life work. That's the Old Way." The Voice was filled with patience, like the voice of a grandfather teaching his grandchild as the two walk together. "Whatever method you choose becomes your master. You've served many masters in your lifetime, but your goal has remained constant. You want nothing more than the Better Life that your experience has taught you is desirable. That goal is your idol. It must be abandoned."

"I-I see your point," the woman replied, though she saw nothing. "Yes, I do believe you're right. Quite right, actually. Your point is revolutionary. I need to find a *spiritual* way. My goal must be God and my method obedience. And prayer. Yes, I must do what's right and trust God with the outcome. You're saying exactly what I've just heard from a wise, elderly woman in my church. She was most interesting."

"She spoke truth to you. But you didn't hear. That's why I've come."

"Well, I think I *did* hear what she had to say." The woman was more indignant than unnerved. "But thank you for coming to reinforce her message. Let's see. Yes, I remember. She told me I was working hard to understand and live by the Principle of Sequence. You know, the idea that *B* follows *A* so that if I want *B,* I must discover the *A* that will bring it about. She was, of course, quite right. I want to know what I must do that will change my life for the better and keep me out of more trouble in the future. She said, too, that I must give up trying so hard and learn instead to pray. Again she was quite right. Of course I must still obey, but since my talk with her, I've been praying far more."

"Why do you pray?" A chill suddenly swept into the room. The woman braced herself against it.

"Why do I pray? What a strange question. I'm certain you know the teachings: Ask and you shall receive; cling to God and don't let go till He blesses you; pester Him, if you must, to get a response; settle for no less than every blessing He has reserved for you."

"That's the Old Way."

The woman frowned. Did the Voice not know the Teachings of the Sacred Book? Then a frightening thought crossed her mind. Perhaps the person behind the Voice knew the Teachings but didn't believe them. Was she speaking with a demon? A false prophet? Was a serpent in the room with her?

"How can that be?" she retorted with strengthened indignation. "My life is difficult. It's right to pray. Why, I run to God with everything. Surely you aren't telling me that prayer is the Old Way."

"Prayer is not the Old Way. *Your* prayer is."

The woman began to cry. "Why do you mock me? I'm desperate. I thought you were going to show me a new way to live. All you've done so far is to make me lose what little hope I had left."

"Your desires are too weak. Small affections create idols, unworthy gods to whom you sacrifice your life. Your prayers are idol worship. You've been bound to your desire for the Better Life, which you define by your experience of pleasure and pain. I've come to show you the New Way that leads to the Better Hope."

The woman's tears intensified into sobs. The sobs turned into wailing. "I only want to do what's right so I can enjoy God's blessings. Is that so wrong? Why won't you tell me what I must do?" If this Voice was from God, she was sure her wailing would cause Him to take pity on her and tell her what to do.

The Voice said, "You want to know what's *effective*. You aren't asking to know what is *holy*."

The woman's wailing quieted. "Are they two different things?"

"Your search for an effective way to the Better Life will lead you to follow the basic principles of this world and not the paths of holiness. Following those principles can sometimes make your life more pleasant, but it can never fill your soul. It will never bring you into the Better Hope.

"Moreover, your determination to do what's effective is futile because you are sovereign over nothing. You control nothing. The Law of Sequence guarantees nothing."

"Are you saying *nothing* I do affects what happens in my life? That I have no influence at all?"

"*Influence* is real. It brings the joy of responsibility and impact. *Control* over what matters most is an illusion. Be grateful you have none."

The woman began to feel different, like a grandchild who just realized her grandfather was wise. To this point her dialogue with the Voice had been a debate. Now she began listening to learn.

The Voice continued. "The illusion of control brings requirement, requirement creates pressure, and pressure leads to slavery, the slavery of having to figure out life to make it work. Those who hold on to the illusion of control lose the enjoyment of freedom."

"I'm not sure I understand. Don't good parents raise good children? Don't faithful tithers enjoy the promise of financial security? Aren't the prayers of God's children always answered by their loving Father?"

"As the Master wills. He is sovereign over all. Be careful never to claim promises He hasn't made. Those who make that mistake think that by doing right they obligate the Master to bless them according to their understanding of the Better Life."

Now the Voice became infinitely gentle. "My child, you're in bondage to the Law of Linearity, what the wise, elderly woman called the Principle of Sequence. It obligates you to do what's right to win the blessings you desire. That law is no longer the guiding rule for God's children. It has served its purpose. The conclusion is clear. By right doing, no one can gain the Perfect Life later nor the Better Life now. By the Master's grace, that law has been replaced by the Law of Liberty. Under the Law of Liberty, you're free to live in the mystery of trust.

"But you haven't accepted the authority of this new law because it requires you to give up the illusion of control. You've cheapened the requirements of holiness by assuming you can do enough right things to bring about the Better Life. Sometimes that works. Sometimes it doesn't. You therefore live with uncertainty and pressure, and you demand to know the way to live that will make your life work as you want.

You maneuver; you do not trust. You negotiate; you do not worship. You analyze and interpret to gain control over what happens; you do not depend. You seek the Better Life of God's blessings over the Better Hope of God's presence."

The woman felt as if waters were about to rise above her head. "But I *do* want my life to work. I've been so miserable. I have to know what I'm doing wrong! Won't you please tell me what to do?"

"Seek only the blessing of His presence, and you'll know what to do. It will fill your soul with joy."

"But...only God's blessings bring me true joy. I need to know how to get them!"

"It's not so. You need only God."

"But I thought I needed God because only He could make my life better."

"When the Master walked this earth, He withdrew from people who wanted to use His power to arrange for the Better Life. He will not be used in the service of weak affections. There's a Better Hope than what you believe is the Better Life. The New Way will take you there."

Those were the last words spoken by the Voice. As soon as they were said, the woman lost consciousness. She reentered time.

The clock's digital display showed 6:30. Morning had come. The woman rubbed her eyes. The question she'd gone to sleep with was still present as she faced the new day, but it no longer seemed urgent. She still didn't know what to do to make her life better, but it didn't seem to matter as much. She was aware of a desire for something, something more than the blessings of the Better Life. *But nothing I can do,* she told herself, *will bring it about.*

A pressure that had long been sitting heavily on her soul was lifting. She felt lighter, more at rest. *Is this what I've been after all along?*

She turned her head toward the window to see the morning sun. As she did, she heard a familiar voice whispering, "You're about to discover the New Way to live." Strange, she thought. It was the voice of a wise, elderly woman.